COME WALK WITH ME

A Journey into Intimacy

By

JACQUELINE VARNEDOE

With

MARGIE KNIGHT

Come Walk With Me
By Jacqueline Varnedoe
Copyright ©2009 Jacqueline Varnedoe

Unless otherwise identified, Scripture quotations are from the *New King James
Version* copyright ©1979, 1980, 1982, 1988 by Thomas Nelson, Inc. Used by
permission. All rights reserved.

Quotations designated (NIV) are from THE HOLY BIBLE: NEW INTERNATIONAL
VERSION®. NIV®. Copyright © 1973, 1978, 1984 by International Bible Society.
Used by permission of Zondervan Publishing House. All rights reserved.

ISBN 978-0-984312108

Writer/ Publishing & Design Director: Margie Knight
                                KnightWriter~2~Publish
                                Denton, TX
                                knightwriter2publish@gmail.com

Cover and Interior Design: Joy Kusek
                                Denton, TX
                                joykusek@gmail.com

Worldwide Distribution
Printed in Canada

ENDORSEMENTS

"I love Jacqueline Varnedoe's approach to hearing and walking both with God and walking out God's Word to us. She grounds it in relationship, something that most have missed. This book is a must read because when we walk with God out of a relationship of love and trust, the results are phenomenal and transforming. Faith comes easy because we know to Whom we have committed ourselves. We trust Him. We do what He says. He is love. We begin to affect everyone around us with heaven's perspective. They too are transformed. Varnedoe, herself, marvelously models what it means to *Come Walk With Me.*"

Barbara J. Yoder

Senior Pastor & Lead Apostle, Shekinah Christian Church
Founder & Apostolic Leader, Breakthrough Apostolic Ministries Network
Chancellor, Breakthrough Leadership Institute (BLI/WLI)

Ann Arbor, MI, USA

"I have known Jacqueline Varnedoe for many years. She is a godly woman who has walked close to God. For years she has taught and demonstrated hearing the voice of God. This book will not only educate your mind, but enable you to walk closer to God, hear the voice of God for yourself and minister the prophetic voice of the Lord to others. Bless you, Jacqueline, for blessing the Body of Christ with this wonderful book."

Dr. Bill Hamon

Bishop of Christian International Ministries Network (CIMN)
Author of *Prophets and Personal Prophecy* and many other major books
Santa Rosa Beach, FL

DEDICATION

To my husband
Heeth Varnedoe III
For his love, support,
and strength.

Your encouragement has caused me
To rise up and be that
Woman of God
I was called to be.

ACKNOWLEDGEMENTS

Margie Knight: Words cannot express my gratitude to you for your excellent writing and editing skills that made the impossible possible.

Bishop and Evelyn Hamon for your love and care through the years.

Dr. Chuck D. Pierce for giving us fresh vision and much encouragement.

My immediate family for their love and encouragement: **Jacqueline and Robert, Rand and Elizabeth, Heeth and Susan, and Howard and Dawn**. You are still my jewels.

My Grandchildren: For your love and many hugs.

Marc and Libby and all our friends at Hunter's Point Celebration Center for all your prayers concerning this book.

Prophetic Leadership Team at New Covenant for your encouragement and prayers while writing this book.

FORWARD

In *Come Walk With Me … A Journey Into Intimacy*, Jacqueline Varnedoe has developed the template for our success as we enter into the crisis time that is manifesting in the world around us. She takes us on a wonderful journey of having ears to hear God's voice, receiving the richness of His love, and operating in the fullness of His power. All three of these components are a must to understand if we are going to walk triumphantly into the future.

To have a future, we must have an intimate relationship with the Lord that allows Him to communicate fresh strategies for victory. We find a good example of this principle when we look at the life of David. In 2 Samuel 5, David initially defeated the Philistines. The Philistines regrouped and came against him once again. The Lord told David to listen for the wind in the mulberry trees and then attack by not pursuing, but coming around from behind. This was a different strategy than what had been used in the previous battle. You can't win today's battles with yesterday's revelation. If David had used the same method in his new battle that had previously brought him victory, he would have ended in defeat.

I am a warrior in the Kingdom of God. Some of you might ask the question, "Why then is a book on intimacy appealing to you?" Jacqueline is a person I know well -- long enough to know that what is written here is reality. Not only is she a woman who can communicate her walk with God, she is a woman of wisdom. Wisdom dismantles the demonic.

Intimacy is a close, familiar, and usually affectionate or loving personal relationship with another person or group. However, intimacy can also be a close association with or detailed knowledge of a place, subject, or period of history. Intimacy is linked with liberty. We war for liberty. To be liberated spiritually takes an embrace from the LORD who will pour His love and grace on you in ways that no other person in any relationship can express. When you are intimate you share secrets with the one you are intimate with. In return, secrets are then shared with you that will produce victory in your life.

Proverbs 4 tell us that we are to be seekers of wisdom. In fact, verse 7 in The Living Bible says, *"Getting wisdom is the most important thing you can do!"* There is no way we can hear the voice of the Lord without drawing near to Him. The primary way of doing this is through worship and prayer. Without making a commitment to seeking God in these ways, we will never be able to gain an understanding of His wisdom. It is from a place of intimacy that we can tap into all of God's covenant promises for us. But like any covenant, if we don't hold up our end of the deal, we will not reap the full benefits of the covenant. If we don't seek a true and intimate relationship with God, we will not be postured to hear His voice when He speaks to us. Therefore, we will not have access to His wisdom and strategy for moving forward.

We are in a season of a new wineskin forming in the Kingdom of God. New wineskins are the new structures where the Spirit of God will release and flow His revelation or wine. In the process of renewing our wineskins, certain things must be restored to us in order to make the process complete. The most important is that He **restores intimate contact with Himself and then produces new relationships with those who will walk together into the future.** Relationship is difficult for many Christians simply because our society breeds fear of intimacy. We protect ourselves. We don't want to get hurt. We don't want to allow our emotions to be seen. And to complicate matters, those who have experienced broken relationships in the past don't want to chance future intimacy. But the simple fact is that we need one another. We need God. Without one or the other, we will never enter into the fullness of restoration. We must begin to allow God to make us intimate communicators with Himself and then each other.

In this book on intimacy, Jacqueline helps us reform our relationships. She reveals to us the importance of intimacy being first. We need to embrace an intimate relationship with God and hear His voice now. The classic analogy of intimacy is Mary and Martha (see Luke 10:38-42). We get so caught up in what we are to do that we forget what we are about. Mary sat at the feet of Jesus until she knew her destiny. Once she knew the purpose of her life, then she could go do the dishes with Martha, or anything else that needed to be done. She did not neglect the task. Through intimacy, Mary simply gained what she needed for her life and then tended to the business of the house. God is calling us into a new intimate place. From this intimate place, we gain our new strategies for moving ahead.

Intimacy is not for ourselves alone. Just as God wants to restore us as individuals, He is equally interested in restoring us as the Bride of Christ. This is a book for the corporate season that we have entered at this time in Kingdom history. For that reason, we must allow Him to bring us into intimate relationships with one another that will thrust us forward into our biblical destiny.

Like it or not, we are in a war that began the day we got saved. On that day we were taken from the kingdom of darkness into the Kingdom of light. Those two kingdoms are violently opposed to each other. Anything that God has ordained us to accomplish is going to be met with resistance from our enemy. Therefore, Satan has set himself against God's destiny for us. In order to reach our full potential in God, we must learn warfare. Sometimes, however, warfare is not as aggressive as it sounds. Warfare through intimacy is important to learn. Through His knowledge you can stop your enemy from stealing God's best from you. At times, however, we must enter into warfare prayer. Therefore, when we are in an intimate place with the Lord, He will begin to give us the strategy we need to defeat the enemy in whatever battles we face. Personally, I don't war just to war. God has set me in His abiding place (see Ps. 91). When the enemy tries to prevent me from getting into or attempts to pull me out of my abiding place, then he and I go to war. I worship the One who can give me victory. My intimacy with Him assures my victory.

This book is filled with worship. Worship, both corporate and private, is a key discipline to maintaining spiritual life. Worship is that place where we can come into intimacy with God. It is not just singing songs, although music can be a catalyst for expressing deep worship to the Lord. Worship is a lifestyle of focusing our minds and hearts on God and all that He is. It is a response to all He has done for us. It is a fragrant, flowering offshoot of our covenant relationship with Him. Many, many things in life are worship issues. In fact, every discipline we have mentioned can be an act of worship, because these disciplines give reverence and honor to God and can bring intimacy with Him.

This book will help you in these crisis times to begin to secure your portion. Jacqueline, along with Margie Knight, has defined the shadow of His Hand over us. They have captured the concept of ABIDING IN HIM! Psalm 91 is rich with promises for those who *"dwell in the secret place of the Most High."* It not only speaks of the unfailing protection we enjoy from the enemy of our souls, but it also speaks of our authority to tread upon the enemy, angels keeping charge over us, deliverance, honor, a long and satisfying life and salvation. These are all promises of the covenant we have with God when we remain in the abiding place of intimate relationship with Him. Remembering that the greatest part of our inheritance is God Himself, we must take this place of intimacy seriously if we are to fully possess our portion.

This book is for men, women, the next generation, business people, and homemakers as well. *Come Walk With Me* captures the call and heart of God for each one of us who want to win our wars ahead. Enter into your journey with Him as you read this wonderful example of relational, intimate contact with the God of the Universe.

Chuck D. Pierce

President, Global Spheres Inc.

President, Glory of Zion International

Harvest Watchman, Global Harvest Ministries

TABLE OF CONTENTS

INTRODUCTION

My walk with the Lord has been a progressive journey just as yours has been. Each of us is at a different stage in our understanding of His Word and in discovering the destiny of our calling and purpose in life. Our growth and maturity continues day by day. In other words, the journey never ends.

Several years ago my husband, Heeth, and I were visiting with friends around our breakfast room table. One of them said to me, "Jacqueline, you really should write a book on intimacy with the Lord. That has been your heart ever since I have known you." My first thought was, *No thank you – not me. Let others write books!*

Sometime later as my youngest son and I sat on the beach enjoying a special family gathering, he said, "Mom, Dawn and I think you should write a book on communion with the Lord." Again, I smiled and tossed the thought aside.

As time passed, I began to have more words of confirmation that I was to write this book, I finally said, "Lord, if this is You, then I am willing."

My next big question was, "Lord, how do I begin?" Then I reflected on the fact that many people want a closer walk with the Lord but don't know where to begin. The comparison that crossed my mind was two families packing to go on a trip together. Each family places different items in the suitcase depending on their individual needs and interests. There will also be some similar items needed and wanted by both families.

So it is in those walking with the Lord. Some of the gifts, disciplines, and commitments I choose to exercise may not be for everybody. The Lord gives each of us different gifts, talents and personal callings. We must be able to recognize and then be willing to choose those things that the Lord uniquely desires for each of us.

My prayer is that you will not stumble over my agenda but continue on your own journey into intimacy. Abba Father is waiting for you. He is calling to you saying, "Come walk with Me. Let me show you how much I love you and want to fellowship with you."

Chapter 1

DISCOVERING THE MISSING LINK

And you will seek Me and find Me, when you
search for Me with all your heart.
Jeremiah 29:13

Have you ever asked yourself, "What am I missing?" Or, perhaps you have come to the end of a day and said, "There has to be more to life than this!"

Most of us have experienced that frustration and sinking feeling at some time in life. It was just that sort of event that a number of years ago started me on a journey to find the missing link in my Christian walk. Little did I know how my life would change as this quest unfolded.

A FULL LIFE YET UNFULFILLED!

A close friend and I had just finished drying the last dish after a large dinner party we had co-hosted. We looked at each other and said, "There has to be more to life than this!"

Both of us had been raised in Christian homes and were very active in our churches, but looking back, we were definitely not "seeking first the kingdom of God." Our lives were full but we were not feeling fulfilled.

Another friend called after the dinner party and invited me to a ladies' group at her home. As I listened to the speaker's testimony that morning, nothing really hit me until in her closing prayer she said, "Lord, I know that You brought each person in this room here for a particular reason." At that moment, it was like a sword pierced my heart, and I knew this was a divine appointment for me.

I went home that day, stood at my kitchen sink and said, "Lord, I give You my heart. Whatever You desire for me to do, I yield to You!" I had no idea where that prayer would lead, but I knew that the Lord had called me to a different walk with Him. The old way had not brought peace or joy, only disillusionment.

A HEART NOT TUNED TO HOLY SPIRIT

My search began with reading *The Cross and the Switchblade* by David Wilkerson that had been mentioned at the meeting. I was intrigued by the part about how the baptism of the Holy Spirit had radically changed David Wilkerson's heart. I knew I had found the missing link in my Christian walk – my heart was not in tune with the Holy Spirit.

Later, after talking with a friend and her husband to get instruction on how to pray for and receive the baptism of the Holy Spirit, I went into my den that night. My prayer was simply, "Lord, I need more of You. Here I am. Please fill me afresh with Your Spirit."

This was when my new journey with the Lord truly began. Did I understand fully what had happened? Absolutely not! However, I did know that I would never be the same again.

KNOWING GOD - THE SEARCH BEGINS

I had been in church all my life but really did not *know* the Lord as a Person, as my Confidant, as my Friend, and certainly not as the Lover of my soul. I began searching the Scriptures and reading many wonderful Christian books written by people, such as Catherine Marshall and Corrie Ten Boom, who had learned to walk with the Holy Spirit in a personal way. What I learned was that I knew a lot about religion but very little about having a true relationship with God as my heavenly Father, as my Savior and Friend, and, especially, as my Helper and Comforter through the Holy Spirit. What I discovered in my journey was that to *know* Him is to love Him and to desire to love and commune with Him more each day.

One of my favorite scriptures that the Lord highlighted for me in the beginning of my journey is Jeremiah 29:13: "*And you will seek Me and find Me, when you search for Me with all your heart.*"

If it is your heart to truly *know* God in a way that will move you into your true destiny, I invite you to take a journey with me in the coming chapters. Remember, we're not walking alone. He is right here with us showing us the way, and nothing can separate us from His love. Get ready for an exciting journey that begins with walking in great grace.

Chapter 2

WALKING IN GREAT GRACE

Ruler of heaven, creator of my heart.
Called to Your presence, drawn to be set apart.
Losing my life now to gain.
I know you're going to change, the face of my identity.

Great grace will be on me I know.
Great grace will follow where I go.
Great grace You have laid on me.
And forever You have changed the face of my identity.[1]

The words of this song truly reflect the great grace the Lord pours out upon anyone who desires to walk with Him in a new way - fulfilling the destiny for which he or she was created. Such a journey requires a change of heart, humility, and grace to shift into a new way of thinking, speaking, and walking. It takes a willingness to allow God to totally change "the face of your identity."

EXCITED YET UNPREPARED

I wasn't aware of how my choice to seek the Lord in a more meaningful way was going to change everything about my life, including relationships with family and friends. Operating in the baptism of the Holy Spirit was not easily understood or accepted at that time. I was so excited about what had happened to me that I wanted everyone to experience the joy and peace I had found.

My husband, Heeth, had been out of town on a business trip when all this took place. So, was he ever in for a surprise when he returned! Looking back, if I had it to do over again, I would have used more wisdom in the timing and sharing of my experience. Instead I met him at the back door and said, "Guess what happened to me? I was baptized in the Holy Spirit and I spoke in tongues."

Heeth was caught completely off guard. When he left town, I was just Jackie who loved to have a good time, went to church on Sunday, but didn't talk about God on any other occasion. Suddenly, in my zeal and immaturity he was faced with this strange woman who looked like Jackie but wouldn't stop talking about Jesus and wanted him to go to meetings, read books, and listen to tapes.

Although he supported me in my new walk, in the beginning he certainly did not understand what was happening. How could he? Previously, neither one of us had ever heard of the baptism of the Holy Spirit. Heeth and I were active in a mainline denomination church, and this new path was way outside his comfort zone.

One day Heeth finally announced to me, "I don't want to hear any more about Jesus!"

LET GO AND LET GOD!

I knew it was time to be quiet and pray. Gracefully, I stepped back and quit nagging Heeth about spiritual matters. I had to let go and let God work in Heeth's life. The Lord then began to bring godly men across his path to be a witness and spiritual mentor. Approximately fifteen months later, Heeth prayed for salvation and was filled with the Spirit. God knew exactly the right time for Heeth to find his new identity in Christ.

When I stopped concentrating on trying to change Heeth, the Lord began changing me. In my quiet times, the Lord increased my understanding of His love and compassion. Before I had truly committed myself to the Lord, I had tried to make Heeth "god" in my life. He is a great husband, but he could not fill the void in my life that the Lord was meant to fill.

Our four children were young at this time. Our daughters, Jacqueline and Elizabeth, were nine and seven and our sons, Heeth IV and Howard, were three and almost two. As I began this journey, I was blessed to still have many years to grow spiritually with our children. I always called them my jewels because to me that that is what they are – priceless.

Fireworks on the 4th of July!

The Lord alone knows what each of us needs to take on our journey as well as how and when we will find our destiny. Jesus warned us that we would face testing and tribulation when we walk with Him.

> *These things I have spoken to you, that in Me you may have peace. In the world you will have tribulation; but be of good cheer, I have overcome the world.*
>
> John 16:33

The word "tribulation" in Greek is *thlipsis*, which can be defined as pressure, oppression, stress, anguish, tribulation and adversity, affliction, crushing, and distress.[2] *Thlipsis* is like spiritual bench-pressing. The word is used for crushing grapes or olives in a press.

After the excitement of being filled with the Holy Spirit, I soon learned what Jesus was referring to in John 16:33 about tribulation. Sometimes I would think, *What is happening? This is like fireworks on the Fourth of July.* We definitely needed great grace at times.

NEW RELATIONSHIPS TO GROW WITH

It is one thing to have an experience with the Lord, but no matter how great the experience is, we must continue the journey of walking and growing with Him. So for me, the big decision was – what do I do next? There was a ladies' prayer group meeting every Tuesday. However, I played tennis on Tuesdays. Big decision time… This was the first step – with many to follow – of having to decide between the good and the best. Playing tennis had been a good thing, but the prayer group was the best place for me at that time.

This was a decision I never regretted. I needed the instruction and mentoring that I received in this group. For more than two years we were blessed with great teaching on how to live the Christ-centered life. We prayed, laughed, and cried together – knowing this was the journey we wanted to take – but it was not always easy. Many in our circle of friends and even family thought we had gone "off the deep end" as the expression goes.

As Heeth joined me on this journey, we were so excited about the things of the Lord that we did not always share things with wisdom. Unfortunately, some of our close friends turned away from us. However, I have to remind myself even today that God is bigger than my mistakes.

Heeth held a high-level executive leadership position with a large company in our community. The head of the company got wind of what was happening in our lives and was not pleased with what he was hearing. This was thirty plus years ago, and people in this small, conservative community didn't know very much about the spiritual renewal we were experiencing. Heeth was called into the chairman of the board's office to discuss the matter. The chairman, W.H. Flowers, said, "I'm real concerned. You're a key man in this organization, but I can't have any religious fanatics running around." Mr. Flowers suggested that Heeth and I should just "calm down" a bit.

Heeth understood Mr. Flower's concern. In an excerpt from Heeth's book, *Called to Excellence,* here is how Heeth responded:

> "I know now that he had a legitimate concern that I would become so completely wrapped up in religion I would let my work slide. As a manager, I've seen it happen to others over the years. At the time I was really nervous. I loved my job and I needed a paycheck. Yet, I knew that what was happening to me was real and that I did not want to compromise my beliefs. I simply couldn't back off from what God told me to do. I explained this to Mr. Flowers and added, 'If I ever do anything to embarrass you, or if I ever don't do what I'm supposed to do on the job, I'll leave.' This was my way of letting him know that even though I felt compelled to be bold in my faith that I intended to do it with wisdom. I think that is what he was trying to tell me he wanted also. And that's where we left it. He never mentioned it again."[3]

Fortunately, Mr. Flowers saw the sincerity in Heeth and allowed him to stay with the company. Under Heeth's leadership the company prospered. Without preaching, Heeth was able to plant seeds of hope in people's lives – hope in the One who never changes.

Heeth and I had the joy of going to dinner with Mr. and Mrs. Flowers years later. During the meal Mr. Flowers looked at Heeth and said, "I am so proud of you." What a blessing and encouragement that was to both of us.

CHOOSING THE BEST ROUTE

Looking back, I see where the Lord closed some doors in our lives because we were not mature enough to walk in those situations. It was not that those situations or relationships were necessarily wrong, but they just were not right for us at that time. It is like going on a trip. There are several possible routes to take. The decision has to be made whether to take the fastest way, the way with the least traffic, or the scenic route. When we come to a fork in the road in life, the choice is ours: Do we choose His way or our way? Others may choose a different route, but we must hear what the Lord is saying to us individually.

FINDING A NEW FRIEND

Honestly, there were some lonely times for me because I am such a people person. I loved my friends and the rejection of some of them was very painful. However, the Lord used it all for good, because it caused me to push into Him in a way I might not have otherwise. The Lord put a hunger in me for His Word and for spending time with Him. He truly became my best Friend during this season. I so wanted to know Him more intimately, though at the time I didn't really know what that meant.

This early portion of my journey was an important time for me as I took those first baby steps into the joy of knowing Him better. It was like a baby taking her first step with uncertainty but determination.

God gave us the grace to walk through the transitions and changes He was orchestrating in our lives. The words of the song, *Great Grace,* were fulfilled in us as He "forever changed the face of our identities." However, we never could have made it to where we are today if the Lord hadn't also given us faith for the journey that stretched before us.

Chapter 3

FAITH FOR THE JOURNEY

"We do not need a great faith, but
faith in a great God."[1]
Hudson Taylor

Faith is a necessity for anyone facing the trials of everyday living or the tribulations Jesus spoke of in John 16:33: *"These things I have spoken to you, that in Me you may have peace. In the world you will have tribulation; but be of good cheer. I have overcome the world."*

The fact most of us fail to recognize is that Jesus wants us to be at peace and to be of good cheer, because He has *already* overcome the obstacles or trials we are looking at with our natural eyes. In other words, Jesus is telling us that faith in a great God will bring peace to our souls.

BUILDING NEW LEVELS OF FAITH

As Heeth and I pressed forward on our journey into a closer walk with the Lord, God was at work building our faith to new levels. Heeth traveled on business quite frequently, and with four children at home, this was sometimes difficult. Crisis with one of the children seemed to happen whenever he was away.

As Howard, our youngest son, was learning to talk, his speech was not clear. We thought he would grow out of it, but when that didn't seem to be happening, we put him in speech therapy. After several months, the therapist said, "Howard is too smart not to be making progress; I think you should take him to a neurologist."

Heeth was out of town when the neurologist's report came back. The diagnosis indicated that the part of the brain that controls speech was damaged, like someone that has had a stroke. The brain knows what it wants to say but has difficulty communicating it to the tongue. Of course, we were both concerned as we discussed the report long distance.

PRAYING THE WORD

Heeth hung up the phone and began to pray for Howard. He went to the Scriptures and was impressed to turn to Mark 7:33-35.

Verse 35 said, "*Immediately his ears were opened, and the impediment of his tongue was loosed, and he spoke plainly.*"

Faith dropped into Heeth's heart at that moment, and he knew that Howard would be healed. Likewise, faith was stirred in my heart when he shared it with me. We spoke that Word out loud for Howard's healing and decreed it on his behalf. We knew it was important to declare it because Romans 10:17 says, "*So then faith comes by hearing, and hearing by the word of God.*" We didn't see any immediate change, but we knew Howard's healing was settled in heaven and on the earth.

WALKING OUT THE PROMISE

At the recommendation of the neurologist, we enrolled Howard in an extensive speech therapy program. This required Howard and me to travel 56 miles round trip for each session. However, what could have been a very difficult time was a great time of bonding for us. He loved hard candy so a little bit of candy went a long way in helping to motivate him to practice his speech. Within one year, Howard was dismissed from the therapy program totally healed. The doctor was amazed and said it usually would take five or six years to make such progress. Heeth and I knew our son had been healed by the Lord. Howard's speech is completely clear, and he never struggled with his speech again.

Each of us faces different faith-building experiences in life. What we learn from our trials becomes our testimony to increase our own level of faith *and* to encourage others. It is by faith that we go beyond the here and now and reach for the seemingly impossible. It is by faith that we endure and overcome the hardships of life.

TESTIMONY OF MIRACLES

One person who truly impacted the world with her testimony of faith in the face of unspeakable hardships was Corrie Ten Boom. Her many books testify of how she survived a Nazi concentration camp during World War II. Corrie watched her dear sister die only three days before she was released from the camp. She later found out that her release was due to a clerical error, and the other women her age were executed a week later.

In her book, *Amazing Love,* Corrie shares that in her travels after the war she discovered that "human hearts are amazingly alike"[2] throughout the world. She used the example of radar on a ship locating the image of another ship despite dense fog that made it impossible to see anything across the water. She wrote, "Faith is like the radar that sees reality through the clouds. The reality of the victory of Christ can be seen only by faith, which is our radar. Our faith perceives what is actual and real; our senses perceive only that which is limited to three dimensions and comprehended by our intellect. Faith sees more."[3]

> It is by faith that we go beyond the here and now and reach for the seemingly impossible.

FINDING ABUNDANT RICHES IN CHRIST

Corrie spoke with a group of young Germans after the war about the abundance of riches Jesus has to offer. A few from the group remained to talk with her after the meeting, and one shared how difficult it was to have faith to believe consistently. Corrie explained the truth of Hebrews 12:2 that says, *"Looking unto Jesus, the author and finisher of our faith…"* and encouraged them to look to Jesus whenever their faith wavered.

KNOWING THE GREAT I AM!

It is impossible to walk in faith unless we truly know the great I AM. Even Jesus' disciples had to come into that knowledge. Jesus asked the disciples who men said that He was, and their answer was that people thought He was John the Baptist or Elijah or one of the prophets. When He asked the disciples directly in Matthew 16:15-17, Simon Peter responded: *He said to them, "But who do you say that I am?" Simon Peter answered and said, "You are the Christ, the Son of the living God." Jesus answered and said to him, "Blessed are you, Simon Bar-Jonah, for flesh and blood has not revealed this to you, but My Father who is in heaven."*

Jesus knew that the revelation Peter had was from the Spirit of God. He also knew that some people would not understand the truth and that was why He spoke in parables so many times. For that reason He told His disciples not to tell anyone that He was Jesus, the Christ.

SEEING GOD'S PERSPECTIVE

In that same chapter of Matthew, Jesus went on and predicted His death and resurrection. Peter was so upset he rebuked Jesus for saying this would happen. Jesus then told Peter he was an offense because he was looking at things from man's perspective instead of God's. Jesus then extended an invitation to intimacy to His disciples in this passage:

*If anyone desires to come after Me, let him deny himself
and take up his cross, and follow Me. For whoever
desires to save his life will lose it, but whoever loses his
life for My sake will find it.*

Matthew 16:24-25

Jesus knew that His disciples had to come into the full revelation of I AM, if they were going to be able to fulfill their calling and destiny after He returned to heaven. They had to change their mindsets and move into a new dimension of faith.

TEACHING MYSTERIES – CHALLENGED TO BELIEVE

As Jesus began teaching about it being necessary to eat of the flesh of the Son of Man and drink His blood in order to have eternal life, many of His disciples were offended. Jesus confronted their unbelief and rejection of the Spirit of God who gives life. He knew by the Spirit who would believe and who would betray Him. Many rejected the truth Jesus was speaking and refused to follow Him any longer.

Jesus challenged His twelve disciples and asked if they also wanted to walk away. But Simon Peter responded:

> *Lord, to whom shall we go? You have the words of*
> *eternal life. Also we have come to believe and know*
> *that You are the Christ, the Son of the living God.*
>
> John 6:68-69

Jesus' disciples, except for Judas Iscariot, had come to know and believe in Jesus as the great I AM. Their faith level had shifted and they did not depart from Him. Those who came to know Him as I AM believed as these scriptures attest:

> *You are from beneath; I am from above. You are of this*
> *world; I am not of this world. Therefore, I said to you*
> *that you will die in your sins; for if you do not believe*
> *that I am He, you will die in your sins.*
>
> John 8:23-24

> *When you lift up the Son of Man, then you will know*
> *that I am He, and that I do nothing of Myself; but as*
> *My Father taught Me. I speak these things. And He*
> *who sent Me is with Me. The Father has not left Me*
> *alone, for I always do those things that please Him.*
> *As He spoke these words, many believed in Him.*
>
> John 8:28-30

TURN YOUR EYES UPON JESUS

As a child growing up in the Baptist church, there were many choruses and hymns that I loved to sing. One of them was "*Turn Your Eyes Upon Jesus*." The words are perfect for this part of your journey:

Turn your eyes upon Jesus
Look full in His wonderful face
And the things of earth will grow strangely dim
In the light of his glory and grace.[4]

Helen H. Lemmel who wrote "*Turn Your Eyes Upon Jesus*" and more than 500 other hymns was a gifted and professionally trained vocalist. She lived through many heart breaks, including being abandoned by her husband when she went blind as a fairly young woman. When she was 55 years old, she heard someone make a statement that inspired her to write "*Turn Your Eyes Upon Jesus*."

"I stood still," Helen later said, "and singing in my soul and spirit was the chorus, with not one conscious moment of putting word to word to make rhyme, or note to note to make melody. The verses were written the same week, after the usual manner of composition, but nonetheless dictated by the Holy Spirit.[5]

Helen's faith, joy, and enthusiasm never wavered in her 98 years of life. In her elder years when a song would drop into her spirit, she called a friend, no matter what time of day or night, to come to record it before she forgot the words. She lived in a tiny little room and kept a plastic keyboard next to her bed. She said, "One day God is going to bless me with a great heavenly keyboard. I can hardly wait!"[6]

I encourage you to turn your eyes upon Jesus and seek Him with all your heart. No matter where you are with the Lord, determine to move to a new level of faith. Remember as we read earlier in Romans 10:17, "*Faith comes by hearing and hearing by the Word of God.*"

We do not just wake up one day and have great faith. However, as we continue to spend time in the Word and walk in obedience to His will, our faith will grow. The Lord will give you a greater level of faith when you need it most because He is a great God.

Lord, we thank you that you have given each of us a measure of faith. Now, Lord, as we continue our journey, we place our hand in Your hand – knowing that if we stumble on the journey, You are there to pick us up. Just as the father who brought his troubled son for deliverance said to Jesus, "I believe but help my unbelief."

Chapter 4

CHOOSING TO TRUST

Trust in the Lord with all your heart...
Proverbs 3:5a

Trust is a matter of choice. It is impossible to walk in relationship with someone you do not trust. To say that we trust someone when everything is going well is easy, but the real test comes during times of crisis. If you desire to have a closer relationship with the Lord, you must determine in your mind and heart to move to a new level of trust in Him.

In Hebrew the word for trust is *batach,* which is translated – to trust, be confident or sure. In the Greek, one of the words used for trust is *peitho* – to rely (by in word certainty). However it is impossible to truly trust, have confidence in, or be fully assured that you can rely on someone unless you have a relationship with that person who over time has proven his or her faithfulness.

TRUST = RELATIONSHIP

I can quote Proverbs 3:5-6, *"Trust in the Lord with all your heart and lean not on your own understanding, in all your ways acknowledge Him and He shall direct your paths."* However, if I do not know Him as a loving Father, Brother, Savior, Lord and Friend, it will be very difficult to trust Him in hard times. The key is the development of a relationship with the Lord that is growing in love for Him each day *before* the crisis comes.

DANGER WARNING!

Without such daily communication or communion with the Lord, it is too easy to allow our love for Him to become stagnant or lukewarm. In other words, we are in danger of leaving our first love, as the Lord speaks to the Church of Laodicea in Scripture:

> *I know your works, that you are neither cold nor hot. I could wish you were cold or hot. So then, because you are lukewarm, neither cold not hot, I will vomit you out of My mouth.*

Revelation 3:15-16

Nevertheless I have this against you, that you have left your first love.

Revelation 2:4

Knowing Him must be a top priority in our lives. You never know when it will be necessary to draw upon your relationship with Him, perhaps even to the point of life or death.

> Knowing Him must be a top priority in our lives.

TRUSTING IN TOUGH TIMES

Our family has faced a number of such critical situations over the years. Our grandson, Randolph Augustus Malone V, was in a serious accident when he was six. He was sitting beside his brother on a low-boy trailer carrying a large farm tractor. When the trailer was pulled around a leaf pile, the leaves pushed Rand's leg underneath the wheel. In an instant he was pulled off the trailer and run over with its full weight crushing his ribs and puncturing his lungs.

Our son-in-law, Rand's dad, who is a physician, witnessed the accident and jumped into action immediately, checking to be sure his neck wasn't broken and reviving him when he stopped breathing. Our daughter arrived on the scene right after it happened, and she prayed fervently all the way to the hospital.

When Heeth and I received the telephone call about the accident, we were two-hours away from Tallahassee attending a wedding. As we drove to the hospital in the midst of our tears, we prayed. I had been studying the Psalms, and the Lord brought back to me verse after verse to pray and declare over our precious grandson. Deep in our hearts we knew that Rand V was in the Lord's hands as was our daughter, Elizabeth, and her husband, Rand IV. Although, we didn't know what the outcome would be, the trust in our hearts assured us that God was there with all of us during those critical days in intensive care.

Randolph V lives today because of God's faithfulness, the prayers of many people, and a dedicated and gifted medical staff. Rand's first request after a time of recuperation at home was, "I want to be baptized in water and receive the baptism of the Holy Spirit." So, on Resurrection Sunday that is exactly what happened. He was baptized in our swimming pool by our pastor, Barry Perez, and was prayed for and received the baptism of the Holy Spirit. He was seven years old at that time. Rand's life is a miraculous testimony of the power of God to heal and to save.

DEFEATING CANCER

A few years later, Heeth was diagnosed with prostate cancer. Our practice through the years in such situations has been to pray and seek the Lord for direction. First, we know He is the Healer because by His stripes we are healed. We know that He performs miracles, with or without medication or medical intervention. However, we, also, believe God uses doctors and medicine to heal. So, after much prayer, we were directed to Dr. Frey Marshall at Emory Hospital in Atlanta. Heeth had surgery and is cancer free today. God's plan is different for each person so it is important to seek the Lord individually. In this case, surgery was God's way of healing for Heeth.

ANOTHER FAITH TRIAL

In June 2005 a two-year period of severe physical testing began for me. While preparing for a family dinner, I began having tremendous pain in my upper back. It was so bad I had to lie down to get relief. After a few minutes, the pain subsided, and I was able to continue getting ready for the evening.

After this happened several times on different occasions, I called my physician. Following a thorough examination, he determined it was a muscular problem and prescribed a muscle relaxer, which did seem to help relieve the pain initially.

GOD IS ALWAYS WITH US!

However, after a trip to Ireland, I began to have back pain as well as chest pains. In August a series of tests led to a heart catheterization. As I was being wheeled to the operating room for the catheterization, I experienced an intense feeling of loneliness. Then almost immediately, I sensed the manifest presence of the Lord. He reminded me that I was not alone. During the entire procedure, it was like the Lord Himself was walking around the operating room. I did not see Him with my natural eyes, but I knew He was there.

After the catheterization, the good news was that heart surgery was not needed. One artery was 40 percent blocked which was treated aggressively with medication.

However, my back pain continued, and I was more and more bent over at the waist. It was becoming difficult to stand for even a few minutes. This was hard to accept because for many years I had been used to walking several miles a day at a fast pace. It appeared I might end up being wheel chair bound if something wasn't done to reverse this progression. We decided to go to an orthopedic surgeon in another city for a second opinion. His diagnosis was not good.

GOD IS ABLE!

Heeth and I drove away from his office feeling like we have been given a big sign which read, "No Hope." Tears flowed as we drove away, but then I said to Heeth, "Our God is able! I refuse to give in to one man's opinion. There is always hope because Jesus is my Healer."

In December I was referred to a physical therapist who finally diagnosed the real problem. The psoas muscle, which lifts the upper leg, was contracted and pulling me over. Why this had occurred was not clear, but at last, we had a reason for the pain. I began five months of intense therapy. Progress was slow with episodes of improvement and then regression. This continued until the therapist finally sent me to another orthopedic surgeon who confirmed the diagnosis but didn't have an answer as to why there was no sustained progress.

After driving to the hospital in Moultrie for therapy, the walk across the parking lot and down the long hall to the clinic seemed like it was a hundred miles each way. It was like carrying a heavy load on my back, much heavier than I could physically carry.

At times after the service ended at our church, I would think, *Lord with Your help I will be able to walk out of here and get into the car.* Each step was an effort.

Finally my therapist in Moultrie released me to return to Thomasville where I began another long season of therapy with a wonderful therapist. Everyone was doing all they knew to do in the natural to help me get through this pain.

To Trust Or Not To Trust?

I wrote in my journal in June 2006, "I am still having back problems. Cannot stand up straight. Walk very bent over. However, I know that I will eventually be okay. The question is 'What do I do in the meantime? Do I trust Him or not?'"

I chose to trust Him with all my heart. Truthfully, through all of this, God's grace was there for me every day! The words, "He will never leave me not forsake me," were burned into my heart. Yes, there were days when tears would come, but I can honestly say those days were few. Even on the bad days, a deep inner peace prevailed in me, knowing I was not walking through this alone.

HOLDING ON TO PEACE

During this period of time, I attended my 50th high school class reunion. It was humbling to be all bent over and there were some things I could not do. One former classmate even mocked the way I walked. As I watched him walk away, I had to fight feelings of hurt, but it made me realize that one person should not make me lose my peace. In contrast, another classmate was in a wheelchair and his attitude was tremendous. His paralysis had been caused by a slip of the scalpel during surgery ten years before. I thought to myself, *Jacqueline Varnedoe, you have nothing to complain about.*

Today, joyfully I can walk upright. This was a very serious condition and the Lord performed a healing miracle over a two-year period. I continue to work with a trainer to keep my muscles stretched and flexible. People who knew me when I was bent over are amazed when they see me now. I am so grateful to the Lord who truly is my Healer, for all the people who prayed for me, and for the wonderful therapists who used their training and gifts to help me recover.

You might ask the question, "Jacqueline, how would you feel today if you were still bent over?" My answer would be, "It would be very hard, but that fact could not take away from the truth that My God can be trusted."

My favorite definition of *trust* is "to put confidence in" or "rely on." I know that after walking with the Lord for 39 years, I can put my confidence in Him 100 percent of the time. He has never and will never let me down. Does that mean everything works out the way I want it to be all the time? No, not necessarily, but He is there with me through all of it. I once heard a pastor say, "He will bring me the easiest way I will let Him to bring me to the point where He knows that I will be fulfilled."

Some of you may be walking in a very difficult situation, and you may be thinking, *Jacqueline, you really don't understand my situation.* I would say to you, "No, I really don't know or understand your situation, but the Lord does."

Many times we don't understand what it means to trust. We say we want to trust in God, but we aren't willing to open up and be vulnerable before Him. God already knows everything about you and your situation. Likewise, He wants you to know Him intimately so that you run to Him and not away from Him. The only way to know Him intimately is to choose to spend time with Him in prayer, in His Word, and in praise and thanksgiving of who He is, in the good times *and* the bad times. Here is how one author explains this truth. "Trust is not built *before* intimacy. Trust is built *in* intimacy."[1]

EVALUATING WHERE WE ARE

The key to learning to trust is to start from where you are today. You may be angry about something that happened in the past. It may be an unanswered prayer for a loved one or perhaps someone very close to you died an untimely death. Sometimes we are hurt by those in leadership over us or disappointed by how we are treated. Whatever it is, just tell the Lord about it. He already knows it anyway. He desires that you come to Him believing that He cares deeply about every detail of your life.

If I am troubled about something, I go into my living room, where I usually have my prayer time, and say, "Lord, here I am again. I know I should not feel this way about _____, but I do." Then I just talk to Him. By the time I finish, I am ready

> "Keep a clean slate before the Lord."

to repent about my bad attitude, taking offense, or whatever it may be. I heard a minister once say, "Keep a clean slate before the Lord."

Sometimes serious situations occur like an unfaithful spouse, a child on drugs, an abusive spouse, or a loved one with a terminal disease; and we need the helping hand of a Christian counselor, a prayer partner, or a support group. Don't let pride keep you from getting the help you need, and remember that isolation is the first step to desolation. We need each other to make it through the tough places. Ask the Lord to lead you to the right person or show you the right strategy to move forward.

A growing relationship with the Lord is a must when adversity comes upon us. He alone can bring that deep inner peace in the midst of difficult circumstances. When I was walking through the two years with back pain, the therapists were excellent, but they could not give me the peace that I needed to face each day.

If you are struggling with trust issues, take a few moments and pray this prayer: *"Lord, I confess that I do not always know how to trust You in everything. Please help me to trust you more each day. I thank You, Lord, that nothing is impossible for You."*

TRUST – A DAILY JOURNEY

Learning to trust is a daily journey. It takes place step by step, precept upon precept, line upon line with our wonderful Lord showing us the way. The Lord is faithful and He will do it if you will simply trust Him.

May our testimony be thus as we continue our journey into INTIMACY:

> *In You, O Lord, I put my trust; Let me never be put to shame. For You are my hope, O Lord God; You are my trust from my youth. By You I have been upheld from birth, You are He who took me out of my mother's womb. My praise shall be continually of You.*

Psalm 71:1, 5-6

Chapter 5

SUBMITTING YOUR HEART IN OBEDIENCE

*Trust and obey, for there's no other way to be
happy in Jesus than to trust and obey.*[1]

As a child growing up in church one of my favorite songs was "Trust and Obey." The words and melody of this song still ring through my spirit. The elements of trust and obedience must work hand in hand if we want to enjoy the peace and happiness of Jesus and His promises.

Many people begin their Christian walk trying to obey a set of rules. They often get so caught up in the "dos" and "don'ts" that they lose the joy of their walk. This is the enemy's way of using legalism and religiosity to hinder the development of an intimate relationship with the Lord. In truth

> Obedience is not a set of rules, it is an act of the heart.

God's Word says, *"I can do nothing apart from His love and grace…"* Obedience is not a set of rules, it is an act of the heart.

The first step, after accepting Jesus as our Lord and Savior, should be to pray: *"Lord, I want to know You – really know You. I don't want just head knowledge about You, I want to know Your heart."* I have found through the years, the more I know and love Him, the more I desire to walk in obedience and do His will.

The word "obey" in Hebrew is *shama,* which means to hear intelligently. In Greek the word "obey" is *hupakauo,* which means to listen attentively. In other words, we must have a listening ear to walk in obedience to His will.

It is important to ask yourself these questions. Am I listening to His voice? Do I truly desire to hear His voice and *do* what He tells me to do?

Looking back on my life, I can remember many times in college when the Lord was nudging me to a closer walk with Him. I went to the prayer room at Huntingdon to pray, but I wasn't listening attentively. I was very much in love with Heeth and would think: *What if the Lord wants me to go to Africa?* I knew that would not fit in with Heeth's plans. Knowing what I do now, I understand the Lord just wanted me to "seek first the Kingdom of God…" I didn't understand that with my obedience and surrender of my will, He would handle the rest and give me the grace to walk it out.

Writing this book has definitely been an obedience issue for me. In the beginning I wanted to shout: "No way! I am not a writer! Let others write books." Then that still small voice I have come to love hearing,

> God sometimes amazes us with His requests.

gently said, "Jacqueline, I am *asking* you to write the book." The choice was mine. He wouldn't punish me or be angry with me if I chose not to write it. However, I do believe He wants to bless my obedience and touch those who will read this book. That is the gracious kind of Father God we serve.

AMAZED BY GOD!

God sometimes amazes us with His requests. Having been called Jackie all of my life, I was surprised when I began to sense that the Lord wanted me to go by my full name, Jacqueline. It did not become evident overnight, but it evolved gradually over a period of time.

I have always kept journals to write down my thoughts and what I believed the Lord was saying to me. In my journal notes I began to notice that the Lord always called me "Jacqueline." I did not think too much about it until Heeth and I went through a time of ministry. We believe that we all need spiritual checkups as well as physical ones on a regular basis. At one session, the minister looked at me and said, "Jackie, I know that you go by Jackie, but the Lord calls you, Jacqueline."

On another occasion during a ministry trip to North Carolina, the ministry team leader turned around in the car and looked at another team member, whose name was also Jackie, and me. Pointing to me she said, "One of you needs to be called Jacqueline on this trip." So, for the next two years as I traveled with this church group from Atlanta, I was called Jacqueline.

THE IMPORTANCE OF A NAME

Very gently the Lord began to confirm that it was His desire for me to be called Jacqueline. In biblical times, names were very important. We read of many occasions where a person's name was changed: Abram to Abraham, Sarai to Sarah, Jacob to Isaac and Saul to Paul. These changes reflected either character changes or major calls from God. In my case, I believe that Jacqueline was the name the Lord had always intended for me to be called by and now was the time to say, "Yes, Lord. I will obey."

Some may think: *What is the big deal about a name change?* Remember, I lived in the same small town all of my life. So, for a woman in her fifties who had always been a people-pleaser, to make a decision to suddenly go by a different name was not easy. Believe me; I had many comments and opinions to overcome. Some old friends said, "I will never call you Jacqueline. You are Jackie to me!" I just laughed and said, "That's fine!"

Heeth, on the other hand, wavers back and forth from Jack to Jackie to Jacqueline. Sometimes when we are speaking, people come up and say, "What *is* your name?" However, for me, it was sheer obedience. I knew the Lord had spoken and it was my choice, to obey or disobey. I made the best choice and obeyed.

PROMPTED BY THE SPIRIT

Another example of personal obedience came when I felt the Lord prompting me to get a master's degree in biblical studies. I had graduated from the University of Georgia with a bachelor of arts degree years before and had taken a number of biblical studies correspondence courses, but never for credit. Again, this was not my idea! As with the name change, I knew the choice was mine.

I enrolled in the Christian International School of Theology and began my study. Over the next few years, I had occasion to think, *Hath God said*? This was the same question Satan used to tempt Eve, and I had many excuses to quit – my mother's serious illness, Heeth's and my travel schedule, grandchildren – but I knew I had a mandate to finish. In 1999, I did receive my master's degree.

OBEDIENCE ENRICHES INTIMACY

One important point I want to make: What is right for one person may be wrong for someone else. God speaks to each of us individually and in different ways. I do not believe that education promotes intimacy, but I do know that obedience enriches

> Obedience enriches intimacy.

intimacy. By obedience we are not earning the Lord's love and approval. We already have that through what He did for us at the cross. However, with our obedience we are saying, "Lord, I desire to do Your will – not my will but Yours be done."

Obedience is equally important in solidifying relationships. All of us have opportunities to take offense against others. Do we choose to forgive and bless those that have hurt us, or do we walk in unforgiveness? The Bible is very clear about forgiveness.

> *And be kind to one another, tenderhearted, forgiving one another, even as God in Christ forgave you.*
>
> Ephesians 4:32

> *Therefore as the elect of God, holy and beloved, put on tender mercies, kindness, humility, meekness, longsuffering; bearing one another, and forgiving one another, if anyone has a complaint against another; even as Christ forgave you, so you also must do.*
>
> Colossians 3:12-13

To forgive is not to condone the sin, as acceptable; to say it made no difference; or to license repetition of it. Rather, forgiveness is a choice: A decision made to no longer hold an offense against another person or group.

FREE TO FORGIVE

As we obey God and walk in forgiveness, it frees us from allowing bitterness to take root in our hearts. A number of years ago I was in a very difficult situation, which produced many opportunities to take offense. At a meeting I heard one of the ladies remark, "I think Jackie has a hard heart!" Her statement was like a sword going into my heart. I knew immediately that it was the conviction of the Lord. I went back to our hotel room and prayed: "Lord, I am so sorry, please soften my heart. Lord, I choose right now to forgive those that have caused me pain."

> Obedience is an absolute must for walking in intimacy.

To this day I have never forgotten how easy it is to allow our hearts to become hard. We have to guard our hearts because such hardness separates us from other people, and, more importantly, it causes intimacy with the Lord to be watered down, causing the fire to go out. Nothing is worth risking that!

Obedience is an absolute must for walking in intimacy. I once heard someone say, "We can have whatever kind of relationship with the Lord we want: It is up to us."

We will be tempted many times to say: "No, Lord, it is too hard. You are asking too much of me. I can't give that up, or I can't stop seeing that person." He will still love us just as He did the rich young ruler in Luke 18:22-23. Jesus said to him, "*You still lack one thing. Sell all that you have and distribute to the poor, and you will have treasure in heaven, and come, follow Me.*"

When the rich young ruler heard these words, he became very sorrowful. He was not willing to give up all of his earthly riches for the sake of the kingdom, and he missed out on the provision and blessings in the present time and for eternity. His lack of trust blinded him from comprehending that with God all things are possible, even replacing all that he would have given up.

The Power of "One Thing"

It is often "one thing" that holds us back in our journey with the Lord. Ask the Lord to reveal to you if there is "one thing" keeping you from taking that next step into a closer walk with Him.

The story of Mary and Martha in Luke 10 is another example of not comprehending the importance of intimacy with the Lord. Martha complained to Jesus that Mary was not helping her serve their guests, because Mary was sitting at Jesus' feet, soaking up His every word.

Jesus answered Martha and said, "*Martha, Martha, you are worried and troubled about many things. But one thing is needed, and Mary has chosen that good part, which will not be taken away from her.*"

It was not that Martha's desire to be hospitable to her guests was bad, but it caused her to be distracted, worried and troubled. This "one thing" kept her from hearing His Word thereby gaining the best "one thing" from being in His presence.

The Lord does everything possible to bless those whose hearts are loyal to Him as we read in II Chronicles 16:9, "*For the eyes of the Lord run to and fro throughout the whole earth, to show Himself strong on behalf of those whose heart is loyal to Him.*" What a joy it is to serve a God that goes to such extreme measures for us. All He asks is that we trust Him with all our hearts.

When the Jewish captives returned to Jerusalem from 70 years of exile in Babylon, the "one thing" God instructed His people to do was to rebuild the temple. These exiles were among the poorest of the Jewish captives who returned, but they quickly rebuilt the altar and began construction on the temple rebuilding. However, over the course of more than twelve years discouragement, opposition from the Samaritans, and preoccupation with other pursuits hindered the completion of the temple.

> Obedience to God involves doing the one specific thing He calls us to do.

Zechariah was called by God to encourage the Jewish people to return to the Lord and His purposes to restore the ruined temple. He reminded them that the Messiah's glory would one day inhabit the temple. However, the fulfillment of the promise of this future blessing was contingent upon present obedience.

Obedience to God involves doing the one specific thing He calls us to do. In Zechariah's day God's command was to rebuild the temple. Today each of us as individuals has a specific plan and call on our lives. Do we obey or disobey? It is obedience in small matters in which we show ourselves to be faithful that allows the Lord to give us stewardship in greater matters.

In the book, *One Thing*, authored by Chuck D. and Pamela J. Pierce, Chuck explains how important it is in a world of chaos not to miss the simple things that usually show us true value.[2]

God will not call us to do something in our own strength and ability.

Chuck shared an example in this book of how the Lord showed him this concept years ago, when he and Pam had taken over the leadership of a Boys and Girls Home that was struggling with many problems. Pam was having some serious health issues that caused her to lose the use of her left arm, and they were stressed by financial pressures.

One night he was so overwhelmed with it all that he made a list with seven major categories. Later that night he went out into the field behind their house to pray. He asked the Lord what he was supposed to do with the issues on the list. He got a clear impression from the Lord that he was to buy Pam a new dress. He only had $67 in their checking account, but he knew God's voice so he added this instruction onto the bottom of his list.

He took Pam shopping, bought her a new dress, and stopped for lunch on the way home. This left only $2, which he put in the offering on Sunday morning, and said, "Lord, me and my list are now Yours."[3]

Pam's arm was healed during the praise and worship that morning and within six months every item on Chuck's list was resolved. Faith takes action and his obedience in doing the *one thing* God told him to do – buy his wife a dress – proved the reality of God's faithfulness.

> God has given us the power of His Holy Spirit to do whatever he asks us to do.

God will not call us to do something in our own strength and ability. Yes, He will use our natural gifts, but it is by His power that we will complete the task as we read in Zechariah 4:6, "*Not by might nor by power* (human ability), *but by My Spirit says the Lord.*"

God has given us the power of His Holy Spirit to do whatever He asks us to do. When we step forward in obedience, the power of the Spirit takes us the rest of the way to complete our assigned task.

We can do this because His way is perfect, His word is proven, and He is a shield about us as it says in this scripture:

> *For you will be my lamp; The Lord my God will enlighten my darkness. For by You I can run against a troop. By my God I can leap over a wall. As for God, His way is perfect; The word of the Lord is proven; He is a shield to all who trust in Him.*

> Psalm 18:28-30

If you have been challenged by this chapter on obedience, pray with me this prayer: "*Lord, You alone know my heart. I do desire to walk in obedience to Your Word, but often I seem to stumble over the 'one thing' You have asked me to do. Thank you, Lord, as I release this desire to You; You will enable me by the power of Your Spirit to continue this journey step by step and precept upon precept. I love You.*"

Chapter 6

DEFINING THE PATHWAY TO INTIMACY

*As the deer pants for the
water brooks, so pants my soul for You, O God.*
Psalm 42:1

Intimacy is not a popular word in today's society. It is probably one of the most misunderstood words in the dictionary. Many people become very uncomfortable with its use, especially in a spiritual connotation. How many times have you read the Song of Solomon? It is probably the least read book in the Bible, and yet it is the most creative, poetic depiction of God's loving character and nature ever to be written.

> Intimacy between God and man was destroyed when sin entered the picture.

God created man in His own image because He desired a relationship with him. Can you even imagine what it must have been like for Adam and Eve to walk in the garden with God and talk with Him face to face?

Intimacy is a legitimate need, but the intimacy between God and man was destroyed when sin entered the picture. Deception by Satan in the form of a serpent successfully tempting man to sin was the cause; but shame, fear, and separation from God were the result. The good news is that the ability for us to walk intimately with our loving God was restored by the shedding of Jesus' blood on the cross, by His death, and resurrection. Jesus paid the price for our freedom and restored all that was lost when sin entered the heart of man. The pathway to intimacy was further opened up to us at Pentecost when the Holy Spirit came to baptize believers with the power and anointing to overcome the enemy. By the Spirit we can once again walk in holiness and in intimacy with the Father. It is our choice to do so.

INTIMACY DEFINED

According to *Webster's New World Dictionary of the American Language*, intimacy is defined as "the state or fact of being intimate;

intimate association; familiarity; or an intimate act; especially illicit sexual intercourse."[1]

To get a better picture of how I believe God would define intimacy, I went to *The Synonym Finder* by J. I. Rodale. Here are some of the descriptive synonyms listed for intimacy: closeness, endearment, familiarity, love, warmth, tenderness, personal, exclusive, special, passionate, innermost, deep understanding, fellowship, confidant,

> **Intimacy is when you allow yourself to be vulnerable.**
> - Cheryl Salem

friendship, companionship, etc.[2] These words express God's character and represent the relationship He desires to have with us. Why wouldn't anyone want to experience such a beautiful, warm and loving relationship described by these words?

"In to Me See"

One of the best definitions of intimacy is shared by Cheryl and Harry Salem in their book, *Being #1 at Being #2*.

> "Cheryl says intimacy is an easy word to say, because when you break it apart it says, 'IN TO ME SEE.' Intimacy is when you allow yourself to be vulnerable. We need to be vulnerable to the Lord and be

> Making the decision to say, "Lord, IN TO ME SEE," is an act of submission.

able to say, 'Lord, I can come before You just as I am. With all the mess and problems in my life, I can allow myself to let down the walls of my heart, to throw back the covers, open the doors, or do whatever I need to do to be vulnerable to You.'"[3]

We have to be willing to say to God, "IN TO ME SEE." We need to be able to say to our spouse and children, "IN TO ME SEE." When we are willing to open ourselves up to scrutiny and be vulnerable, we find our pathway to intimacy clearly opens before us. It will change our relationship with God and will transform our family life as well.

AN ACT OF SUBMISSION

Making the decision to say, "Lord, IN TO ME SEE," is an act of submission. We have talked about trust and obedience in earlier chapters, but submission is a subject not everyone understands. Have you ever seen a child do what he is told to do, but you sense a rebellious or angry spirit boiling under the surface? It is like the child is saying, "I'm sitting down on the outside but inside I'm standing tall." The obedience may be done in fear of punishment for disobeying, but he hasn't submitted his heart to the authority in his life.

THE POWER OF TONGUES

Another key factor to defining the pathway to intimacy is speaking in tongues. In my early journey with the Lord, I learned first-hand how precious it was, as well as how much division it caused in the Christian world. I was even advised not to put this in my book because some Christian bookstores would not sell my book. My response to this is to say that as Christian brothers and sisters, we can agree to disagree. Just let me share with you what joy my prayer language brings me and some personal testimony. Then I'll allow you the freedom to choose for yourself whether it is important to you.

When I first read about speaking in tongues in the book, *The Cross and the Switchblade,* I personally had no negative thoughts. I knew I was searching to have a deeper experience with God, and I said, "Lord, I want more of You and if this is part of Your plan for me, I want it." I knew so little about it that I did not associate speaking in tongues with any group of people or negative beliefs. At that time in my life, I was like it says in Psalm 42:1, "*As the deer pants for the water brooks, so pants my soul for You, O God.*"

Scripturally, tongues were an important part of what took place on the Day of Pentecost when the Holy Spirit was imparted to the apostles and other Christians waiting in the Upper Room as Jesus had instructed them to do.

We can read this in Acts 2:2-4: "*And suddenly there came a sound from heaven, as of a rushing mighty wind, and it filled the whole house where they were sitting. Then there appeared to them divided tongues, as of fire, and one sat upon each of them. And they were all filled with the Holy Spirit and began to speak with other tongues, as the Spirit gave them utterance.*"

BREAKING THROUGH TO GOD'S HEART

Jesus knew that the apostles in the Early Church would not be able to do what He had prepared them to do without the power of the Holy Spirit. Tongues was a very important part of the gifts the Holy Spirit provided. The apostle Paul said, "I wish that you all spoke in tongues as I do." When we don't know how to pray about a difficult situation, tongues are a powerful tool that allows us to break through to the very heart of God.

In his book, *The Hidden Power of Speaking in Tongues*, Mahesh Chavda says, "I believe in the power of speaking in tongues. I believe because I have witnessed its power in my own experience as well as in the experience of others."[4]

The first time Mahesh experienced tongues he said it was like something came bubbling up inside, and he couldn't contain it. He sang in words he didn't understand for an hour and twenty minutes without stopping. Mahesh was fluent in many languages, but he did not recognize the language of the words he was singing. It was like being in ecstasy, and he felt a greater love for Jesus than ever before. He didn't know what had happened and, intellectually, was somewhat embarrassed by it all. Later he explained what had occurred to a Catholic nun in one of his college classes. She explained to him that he had been baptized in the Holy Spirit. His life was never the same again.

> Speaking in tongues carries many benefits for our spiritual lives.

TONGUES BRING REFRESHING

Speaking in tongues carries many benefits for our spiritual lives. The more I speak in tongues, the more I flow as one with the Holy Spirit. When I am exhausted and weary, praying in tongues brings refreshing to my spirit and soul. It is like being in a flowing river on a hot day. Along with delving into God's Word and spending quality time with Jesus on a daily basis, speaking in tongues is one of the best ways to get refreshed.

In an earlier chapter I shared about our son Howard's speech problem. During that season of time while traveling alone, I started praying aloud in tongues as I drove. Then the Lord began to give me the interpretation of what I had been praying in the Spirit. This is what He spoke to me: "Howard's speech will be clear much sooner than the doctors anticipate. He is called by Me and My hand is upon him. As he grows up, he will be above average scholastically and, also, in the honors he will receive." All of this has come to pass. Howard is a testimony of God's faithfulness.

When our oldest daughter, Jacqueline, was in the eighth grade, she fell from her horse. It was immediately evident that her arm was broken, and we were thirty minutes away from the hospital.

Praying in tongues brings edification to our spirits.

Heeth drove while I sat in the back seat with Jacqueline praying for her in tongues. As concerned as Heeth and I were, I knew that the Lord had everything in His hands. By praying in tongues, I knew I was praying the Lord's heart for her.

On another occasion we were out of town for our son's high school football game. Howard injured his leg while playing, and we were once again miles from our doctor and hospital. As we traveled home in our van, perfect peace came over us as we prayed in tongues. Unfortunately, his leg was broken, which meant he was out for the rest of the season. So, things do not always turn out the way we would like, but that did not take away from the peace and strength the Lord gave to all of us as we walked through that time.

EDIFICATION TO OUR SPIRITS

Praying in tongues brings edification to our spirits. Many times when I feel spiritually dry, I just begin to pray in tongues as the Word tells us to stir ourselves up in the Holy Spirit. Of course, praying in tongues is not the only way to be refreshed and refocused, but for me it is the best way.

Does praying in tongues make me a better Christian than someone else or more spiritual? Absolutely not! However, for me that night in our den when I was seeking the baptism of the Holy Spirit, the question was, "Why would I not want everything the Lord has provided for me?" The Lord wants only the best for His children. He alone knows what we need to walk the journey He has called us to walk.

I remember that next day after I received the baptism of the Holy Spirit and spoke in tongues for the first time. I was so excited that I called a close friend and said, "You must read *The Cross and the Switchblade*. It is such a wonderful book." I had interrupted dinner with her family so we didn't talk further. The next morning she came to my house and said, "Jackie, what is going on? It is not like you to call me at night and insist that I read a certain book."

> Man cannot tame the tongue but the Spirit can.

I shared my testimony with her, and she said, "I love you and appreciate what you have shared, but I don't think tongues are necessary." The Lord gave me the wisdom to respond, "Don't let that hold you back. If it is to be part of your experience, the Lord will show you."

Eventually she did receive the baptism of the Holy Spirit and spoke in tongues and became one of the leaders in our prayer group. The key was that she had the freedom to make her own choice, and God visited her at the right time. I did not try to force it on her.

A wonderful Bible teacher came to Thomasville in the early days of our new walk with the Holy Spirit, and he played a great part in our spiritual growth. He told us about a prayer group meeting in his house once a week. As people gathered, they lifted up prayer requests one at a time by praying in tongues until a release came before moving on to the next request. During this time they saw miraculous answers to prayer.

THE POWER OF AGREEMENT

Praying in tongues in unity as a group releases great power and the faith for answers, just as it says in Matthew 18:19-20, "*Again, I say to you that if two of you agree on earth concerning anything that they ask, it will be done for them by My Father in heaven. For where two or three are gathered together in My name, I am there in the midst of them.*"

In James 3:8, we read, "*But no man can tame the tongue. It is an unruly evil, full of deadly poison.*" Man cannot tame the tongue but the Spirit can. I believe that we truly humble ourselves when we say, "Lord, I yield my tongue to You – speak through me both in the natural and in the Spirit." God does hear and answer such a prayer.

I can say this no better than Mahesh Chavda does: "If everything is wonderful in your life, and you are happy and satisfied with all that you have in God, bless you. If, however, you are hungry for more of God, then I urge you to get more of the anointing and power of the Holy Spirit. Speaking in tongues is the hidden key to moving in the power and anointing of the Holy Spirit."[5]

Having shared my heart on this very delicate subject, I hope you will seek the Lord diligently on this matter for yourself. If you decide not to include tongues on your journey into intimacy – please still take the journey. Don't allow anything to distract you from a closer walk with the Lord.

Chapter 7

STEP 1: SEEK THE TRUTH OF GOD'S WORD

Your word is a lamp to my feet and a light to my path.
Psalm 119:105

To discover God's pathway into intimacy is a lifetime journey. It will take you onto paths you may not have walked before, but you are the only one who can uncover the mysteries of God that are hidden along the way just for you. Each person's journey is unique. It is a four-step process of seeking the truth of God's Word, learning to hear God's voice, discovering the power of prayer, and living in the fear of God versus the fear of man. In this and the next three chapters, we will explore these four steps carefully.

STEP #1 – THE TRUTH OF GOD'S WORD

Psalm 119 is the longest Psalm in the Bible, and it provides the best foundational understanding of God's Word and its purposes than any other chapter in the Old or the New Testament. If you study it carefully, your path will truly be illuminated for your journey into knowing God and His ways.

> To discover God's pathway into intimacy is a lifetime journey.

I was blessed to have been raised in a Christian home by parents who lived what they believed. Of course, they weren't perfect, but they "walked their talk" and set our feet on a solid foundation in God's Word. We attended church and Sunday school every week. As a small child I memorized Bible verses, did sword drills – finding verses in the Bible – and had an understanding of who Jesus was and what He had done for me.

In high school I completed a full-year of Bible study with an excellent teacher, Marjorie Stith, who knew the Bible so well that she taught without notes. When she died in her 90s, she was still excited about getting up every morning and reading her Bible. Marjorie taught Bible studies for over fifty years. For her the Bible was as it says in Hebrews 4:12: *"For the word of God is living and powerful, and sharper than any two-edged sword, piercing even to the division of soul and spirit, and of joints and marrow, and is a discerner of the thoughts and intents of the heart."*

At Huntingdon College in Montgomery, Alabama, we were required to take two years of Old and New Testament Theology. So, you might assume I was well versed in the Word. It was true to an extent, but what I had at that time was a lot of head knowledge and very little heart knowledge. There is a big difference.

Apart from knowing the Word, it is impossible to have an intimate relationship with the Lord. We must have, not just head knowledge, but a true heart knowledge of who the Lord is and what He desires for you or me to be and to do.

OPEN MY EYES TO SEE

As I began my walk with the guidance of the Holy Spirit, I felt like I was back in first grade again: learning precept upon precept about who my Father is, what His heartbeat sounded like, how much He loves me, seeing His holiness...the list goes on and on. I was now grasping a picture of the awesomeness of God, not a list of dos and don'ts.

> Apart from knowing the Word, it is impossible to have an intimate relationship with the Lord.

In the early years of our journey, Heeth and I were blessed to go on ministry trips with Lay Renewal teams from the Presbyterian

Church. On one of these trips a very special lady who taught Bible in a college in South Carolina said, "Don't read the Word without first praying, 'Holy Spirit, please teach me as I read and illumine your Word to me!'" Another good prayer she recommended was to pray Psalm 119:18, "*Open my eyes, that I may see wondrous things from Your law.*"

THE WORD THAT COMFORTS

I can think of many times the Word of God has blessed me, comforted me, and sometimes gently rebuked me. One example is found in Psalm 119:50: "*This is my comfort in my affliction, for Your word has given me life.*"

My mother had been seriously ill, and the doctor told us she would probably be gone in a matter of a few months. Heeth and I were on a short ministry trip. He was speaking at a men's meeting, and I was in the hotel room studying for my master's degree. I was very concerned about my mother and was feeling depressed. However, as I began to read and study the Word, it was like the comfort of the Lord flooded over me. By the time Heeth returned to the room several hours later, I was filled with His peace. I was still concerned about my mother's illness, but the Lord had reminded me that He loved mother more than I did, and her life was in His hands. She lived for two more years.

As I spent time in the Word, I still was not one of those people that could quote you chapter and verse of anything you asked me. Yet, I began to get His heart. I have not yet arrived in full maturity, but I am still committed to the journey.

HIDING THE WORD IN YOUR HEART

On another occasion Heeth had spent some time with a young man from church. He asked Heeth for advice about a financial investment opportunity he and his wife had heard was a good way to make extra money. As Heeth shared this with me that evening, I responded, "Heeth, that is not the Father's heart." Heeth had already advised the young man against the investment, but the couple went ahead with it anyway and lost a lot of money. Eventually they ended up in divorce.

The point of this story is not to say they should have listened to Heeth's advice although it was probably sound wisdom at the time. Rather, it is important to have the Word hidden in our hearts as it says in Psalm 119:11: "*Your word I have hidden in my heart, that*

I might not sin against You." Then when important decisions are considered, His Word will convict us to make the right choices.

SEEKING HIS BEST

One of the enemy's tactics is to distract us with good things to keep us from God's best. His best and highest calling is for us to do those things He has purposed for us to do. That is why it is so important to seek first His face and to know Him intimately. As that intimacy evolves, all those things He has appointed for us to do will be birthed in the right time and season. Bible studies are great, church work is needed, lunch with friends, sports, helping others, etc. all have their place. However, it must start with the Lord and me – just the two of us!

> One of the enemy's tactics is to distract us with good things to keep us from God's best.

Discover what works best for you in finding your own secret place with the Lord and get started. No one plan fits everyone. For some, listening to the Bible on CD in the car or in a quiet time each morning or evening is a great way to meditate and be filled. For others, a more structured Bible study plan is more effective. Personally, I let the Lord lead me into a study plan. For example, years ago I felt the Lord wanted me to do an intense verse-by-verse study of the book of Ruth, meditating on each verse and then keeping a journal of the revelation He gave me. The next book I studied was the book of Esther. The treasures I discovered as I stud-

> Condemnation comes from the enemy, not from God.

ied and prayed were wonderful, just like it says in Psalm 119:162: "*I rejoice at Your word as one who finds great treasure.*"

Just Do It!

My advice to you is to pray and what you feel impressed to study, just do it. Start where you are and don't worry about the length of time you are spending or if you miss a day. You won't find any scripture that says you must read the Word for ten minutes or one hour. Condemnation comes from the enemy, not from God.

As you study and meditate on the Word, your mind will be fixed on Him, and He truly WILL keep you in perfect peace as it says in Isaiah 26:3: "*You will keep him in perfect peace, whose mind is stayed on You, because he trusts in You.*" As you delve into His Word on a consistent basis, your path to intimacy will begin to open up before you.

Chapter 8

STEP 2: HEARING THE VOICE OF GOD

My sheep hear My voice, and I know them,
and they follow Me.
John 10:27

In our media-driven world, many critical remarks have been made by members of the news media about those who claimed that God had spoken to them. The very thought that the God who created the universe would desire to speak with us is totally foreign to many people.

The question I pose is this: "Why wouldn't God want to speak to us today?" Just as most natural parents love to interact with their children, even more so, God the Father likes to talk with His children. One of the reasons He created man was so that He could enjoy fellowship with us, and we, likewise, could enjoy Him.

THE HELPER COMES TO SPEAK

In the gospel of John 14-16, Jesus was explaining to His disciples why He was going back to the Father. His instructions to them included the importance of abiding in the True Vine. Jesus tried to prepare them for His coming rejection, but, most importantly, He wanted them to know why the Holy Spirit – the Helper – would come and "speak" to them. The Holy Spirit would cause their sorrow to turn to joy, after His death and His return to the Father.

> It is through the voice of the Holy Spirit that God speaks to us today.

When we first start walking with the Lord, He seems to speak little and seldom. The "pouring out" is on the side of the one seeking to know Him. In John 16:4 Jesus said, "...*And these things I did not say to you at the beginning...*" The Lord has much to say to His children, which cannot be said at the beginning. He first says, "follow me," and draws us away from other interests and other distractions. Then He can begin to tell us of a path that is expedient for us, one leading to a fuller knowledge of Him.

Jesus knew that it was necessary for the Holy Spirit to come so we would be able to hear the "truth" as it says in John 16:13-15: "*However, when He, the Spirit of truth, has come, He will guide you into all truth; for He will not speak on His own authority, but whatever He hears He will speak; and He will tell you things to come. He will glorify Me, for He will take of what is Mine and declare it to you. All things that the Father has are Mine. Therefore, I said that He will take of Mine and declare it to you.*"

OPENING THE COMMUNICATION LINE

We must comprehend that it is through the voice of the Holy Spirit that God speaks to us today. That is why it is so important to be baptized in the Holy Spirit so that the communication line is open to us between heaven and earth.

When we first begin our journey with the Lord, most of our prayer time is spent going down a list of wants or needs. It is truly a one-way conversation. Most of us were not taught to wait and listen to what the Lord might desire to speak to us.

There are many benefits to hearing the voice of God. One key benefit is that it brings revelation of His plans for us. He, also, gives us divine strategies as to how to co-labor with Him.

Each of us has a destiny. Even before we were created in our mother's womb, He called us forth. He has a plan for each of us, but it is our choice to accept His plan or reject it.

> Each of us has a destiny.

In my own life, I thought many things would bring me joy that actually only brought disappointment and disillusionment. Most of those things were not bad things, but I had my priorities mixed up. Over the years God was trying to gently draw me closer to Him, but I would not make that total surrender. When I finally made the decision and said, "Take all of me, Lord," then and only then did my life truly begin to change. I began my journey that would take me to a place in Him – a place where I would find true joy and satisfaction.

THE WAY GOD SPEAKS

The Lord speaks to us in many different ways. It is rarely an audible voice that we hear, although that is possible. God speaks to us in the person of Jesus, who was God Himself manifested in the flesh, the full and complete expression of God Himself. Jesus tore the veil that kept us from entering into His presence. He also removed our dullness of ear so we can hear Him. Those who have received Jesus as their Lord and Savior have received His Spirit and have become the temple of God, a dwelling place for the Most High.

God, also, speaks to us as we read the Bible. The Bible is called the "Logos Word" – the written Word inspired by God. However, while reading the Bible the Holy Spirit may highlight a "Rhema Word" to us. A "Rhema Word" is a specific word for us at a particular time. The best way I can describe it is this: A particular portion of scripture just lights up in your heart, and it speaks to your need or situation at that moment. That is why it is so important to read and study the Word and hide it in your heart, so that in times of need the Holy Spirit can illumine it to you.

> A "Rhema Word" is a specific word for us at a particular time.

If you grew up in church, as a child you might have memorized this verse in Psalm 119:11 – "*Your Word have I hidden in my heart, that I might not sin against You.*"

As I shared in a previous chapter, the Scripture from Jeremiah 29:13 was definitely a "Rhema Word" for me in March 1970. The Lord was promising me that if I would seek Him with all my heart,

I would find Him – not just head knowledge but true intimacy. Today, many years later I can truly say that has happened.

UNDERSTANDING PROPHECY

The Lord also speaks to us through prophets and the gift of prophecy moving in His people. In 1995 after many years of intense training and mentoring, I founded a prophetic school at New Covenant Church in Thomasville, Georgia. We teach the foundational principles of prophecy, instruction on the gift of prophecy, and how to distinguish between the office of the prophet and the gift of prophecy. There are prophets in the body of Christ today. They hear the Lord and bless those they minister to with encouragement, exaltation, and comfort.

Yes, there is a danger of abuse of prophecy. Jesus warned that there would be false prophets. It is the duty of leaders in the church to teach, train, and activate believers so they can learn to distinguish between the false, the true, and the immature prophet.

TESTING THE SPIRITS

However, it is the individual believer's responsibility to test the spirits carefully and use wisdom, not just accepting what is spoken by others as truth. This, also, can be an effective way to test what you might be hearing within your own spirit when faced with an important decision. We are all human. Whatever words come forth from the Spirit are sifted down through our natural minds, which are subject to our fleshly thoughts and desires. Therefore, caution is warranted.

One of the best ways to do this is written in 1 John 4:1-3, 6: *"Beloved, do not believe every spirit, but test the spirits, whether they are of God; because many false prophets have gone out into the world. By this you know the Spirit of God: Every spirit that confesses that Jesus Christ has come in the flesh is of God, and every spirit that does not confess that Jesus Christ has come in the flesh is not of God...By this we know the spirit of truth and the spirit of error."*

A friend tells the story of using this scripture when the Lord identified his mate in a rather supernatural way. It was during a time when the Spirit was being poured out at their church. He had just recently met a young woman from the church who was helping pray for people during the nightly ministry meetings. Joe was traveling to Colorado and as he settled down to read his Bible on the airplane, the Spirit of the Lord spoke to his spirit and said, "I have provided Margie to be your mate."

This was totally unexpected and came as a bit of a shock to Joe. He didn't even know her last name at that time. He instinctively said, "Oh, no Lord."

Then he heard the Spirit say, "Are you going to reject the gift I am giving you?"

Joe was a man of the Word and knew how to test the spirits, especially for such a critical decision. He said, "If this is you, Lord, I need you to tell me that Jesus Christ has come in the flesh!"

In his spirit, Joe heard the Spirit say emphatically, "Jesus Christ has come in the flesh and I am providing Margie to be your mate!"

That settled the matter in Joe's spirit for him to move further into prayer about this relationship. Interestingly enough, when he returned home and spoke with Margie about it, she had experienced a similar unexpected visitation and word from the Lord. After carefully seeking guidance and confirmation from their church leadership, Margie and Joe were married and have been serving the Lord together for more than fifteen years.

DESIRE TO HEAR HIS VOICE

There are many hindrances to hearing the voice of God. Some people, yes, even Christians, have no desire to hear His voice. Jeremiah 6:10 reads, "*To whom shall I speak and give warning, that they may hear? Indeed their ear is uncircumcised. And they cannot give heed. Behold, the word of the Lord is a reproach to them; they have no delight in it.*"

Tradition itself is not a bad thing unless it holds us back from wanting more of God. Heeth and I were teaching at a church in Tennessee. A lady in one of our seminars said, "I made up my mind a long time ago that I wanted no part of prophecy, because that is not what they teach in my church."

Many times people do hear from God until He disagrees with something they may desire to do or not to do. Then they rebel against what the Lord is saying to them. This is a dangerous place to be as Judah's captivity was portrayed in Ezekiel 12:2: "*Son of man, you dwell in the midst of a rebellious house, which has eyes to see but does not see, and ears to hear but does not hear; for they are a rebellious house.*"

> Tradition itself is not a bad thing unless it holds us back from wanting more of God.

Yes, there are times when God speaks and we hear, but we don't want to believe it is Him, because He says things we do not want to hear. That is why we must know and use the "Logos Word" of God so that we can discern between the flesh – the things we want in our self life – and the Spirit – the things God has in store for us if we are obedient.

These Scriptures reveal the blessings of hearing His voice:

Blessed is the person who listens to the Lord and hears. Blessed is the man who listens to me, watching daily at my gates my gates, waiting at the posts of my doors.

Proverbs 8:34

Your ears shall hear a word behind you, saying, "This is the way, walk in it," whenever you turn to the right hand or whenever you turn to the left.

Isaiah 30:21

TUNING YOUR EARS TO LISTEN

As people who are born of the Spirit, it should be normal for us to communicate on a spiritual level as Jesus stated in John 15:15: *"No longer do I call you servants, for a servant does not know what his master is doing; but I have called you friends, for all things that I heard from My Father I have made known to you."*

While we are all called to hear the voice of God, we each hear Him differently. Therefore, we must learn how God speaks to us.

A great way to practice hearing the voice of God is to journal. If you have never done this, journaling is simply getting before the Lord, and then writing in a notebook or typing on your computer what you think the Lord said to you. Remember, not everything you write down will be from the Lord, but you are listening and training your ears to hear His voice.

> While we are all called to hear the voice of God, we each hear Him differently.

If you are a parent, you know how much it means to communicate with your children or grandchildren. My children are grown, but I still love to hear their voices when they call. The Lord is no different. He loves to hear your voice, and He loves for you to take the time to listen to Him. I'm sure He has already been talking with you, but you may not have learned to recognize the sound of His voice.

WISDOM IN SHARING WHAT YOU HEAR

When we start learning to hear from the Lord, a good practice when sharing with others is to simply say, "I sense the Lord saying…" That leaves the door open for others to communicate with you. It is hard to respond to someone when they say, "The Lord told me…"

In a prayer group Heeth and I attend, if someone believes the Lord is speaking to them, they will say, "This is what I sense the Lord is saying… What do you think?" This leaves the door open for others to agree or disagree.

There is no room for pride and arrogance in our walk with the Lord. He turns His face away from the prideful. True humility is born out of an awareness of God's greatness, grows in a heart full of gratitude, and matures in the awe of His passionate love for us. Neither is there room for false humility that manifests from an ungodly case of low self-esteem. We see throughout Scripture that when people get an identity change from God, they are catapulted into the des-

> Learning to hear the voice of God is part of every believer's destiny.

tiny that once eluded them. Learning to hear the voice of God may be a new experience, but it is part of every believer's destiny.

HIS STILL SMALL VOICE!

Often, we expect God to speak in spectacular ways. However, most often He speaks in a still small voice like He spoke to Elijah in I Kings 19:11-12: *"Then He said, "Go out, and stand on the mountain before the Lord. And behold, the Lord passed by and a great and strong wind tore into the moun-*

> God meets us where we are and takes us as far as we want to go.

tain and broke the rocks in pieces before the Lord, but the Lord was not in the wind; and after the wind an earthquake, but the Lord was not in the earthquake; and after the earthquake a fire, but the Lord was not in the fire; and after the fire a still small voice.

When Elijah heard the still small voice, he knew that it was the Lord speaking to him."

When our hearts truly desire to hear His voice, we will hear. As we have already looked at the many ways the Lord speaks to His children, the key to remember is – do not put God in a box. Each person's experience will be different. God meets us where we are and takes us as far as we want to go. So, please continue on the path of your journey. As the old hymn goes, "*He gets sweeter and sweeter as the days go by.*"

Chapter 9

STEP 3: COMMUNICATING IN PRAYER

Rejoice always, pray without ceasing, in everything give thanks; for this is the will of God in Christ Jesus for you.

I Thessalonians 5:16-18

Prayer is the first line of communication with the Lord. Attempting to walk intimately with the Lord without prayer would be impossible. However, people have different ideas or definitions of what constitutes prayer. The Webster's Dictionary defines prayer as "an address to God in word or thought – a set order of words used in praying – a religious service consisting chiefly of prayers." All of these definitions could apply depending on each person's religious background and training. Remember what I said earlier about not putting God in a box? That definitely applies to prayer.

> Prayer is the first line of communication with the Lord.

> It pleases God's heart when generations come together to pray and to worship.

When our children were growing up, I always had prayer time with them before bed and before leaving for school each morning. I have continued the tradition with our grandchildren. One night recently, I was spending time with one of our grandsons and I said, "Do you want to pray or would you like me to?" His answer surprised me when he said, "Momsee, you pray because you pray so pretty." I did pray that night, but the next day I was reflecting on what he said. I didn't want him to think the Lord likes "pretty prayers" better than simple prayers from the heart. So, on that evening as I was telling him good night, I said, "God loves to have you talk with Him as a friend. It doesn't matter how we think it sounds." He prayed and I knew that his child-like prayer touched the heart of God.

GENERATIONAL BLESSINGS

Several years ago when my oldest granddaughter, Morgan was a senior in high school, I was blessed with a special gift. Morgan had been on the tennis team and, therefore, had practice every day after school. However, that spring she came to me and said, "Momsee, I have decided not to play tennis, because I would like to have the time with you once a week after school to pray." What a treasure – a priceless jewel – was that time we had together in prayer. We saw so many prayers answered during those few months. I believe that it pleases God's heart when generations come together to pray and to worship.

TIME TO FELLOWSHIP

Prayer is something we should want to do, not have to do. It is an opportunity to fellowship with the Lord – to truly come to know Him. In the natural we come to know someone as we spend time talking and sharing our hearts together. Even now after 49 years of marriage, Heeth and I take time to sit down and share what is truly going on in our lives. Our marriage could not have grown into the close relationship we have today without spending quality time together. Likewise, we must open our hearts and spend time with the Lord on a continuous basis to have an intimate relationship with Him.

> Prayer is something we should want to do, not have to do.

There are many different ways to pray. Sometimes we need to be with the Lord without any particular agenda. Then there are times to petition the Lord, interceding for others, for our family, and for our nation. This can be done individually and in corporate groups at church or in small prayer groups in homes.

You might ask, "Jacqueline, what do you mean 'spend time' with the Lord?" I can only answer from my own personal experiences. What may be right for me may not work for you. However, I do know this…the Lord will show you His way for you. He alone knows what will best minister to your heart.

I like to begin my day with Bible reading and then just sitting in my living room talking with the Lord. Often I just sit and listen to what He may prompt me to pray specifically for that day. Each day is different. Other times, I pray in tongues for a few minutes and then begin to thank Him for being the faithful God that He is – full of grace and mercy. Some mornings I don't have as much time as I would like, but my heart's prayer is, "Lord, this is Your day and I am Your child. Thank You that You will show me Your way."

> God likes to talk to us whenever and wherever we happen to be.

Pray As You Go!

Although it is good to have a special, quiet place to pray, prayer is not limited to that one location. When your children run in from outside and are excited to tell you something, you don't drag them off to a special room in the house to talk. God likes to talk to us whenever and wherever we

> As you develop a habit of prayer, it becomes a natural instinct.

happen to be. As I move through my day, I pray as I go for specific family needs, church needs, friends, and for issues that are on my heart that day. As the day progresses, I try to stay sensitive to what His voice is saying to me. It is amazing the people He will put on my heart that need prayer.

The best thing about prayer is that you can do it anywhere at any time. It can be a quiet whisper from your heart or a loud and bold declaration. It can be a quick, hurried prayer, or it can be a long, intense time before the Lord. The key is to just do it! As you develop a habit of prayer, it becomes a natural instinct. Distractions and busyness will happen but don't get on a guilt trip about it. This is a journey and sometimes we get on the wrong road, but the Lord is always there to point us back to His way, if we just ask and listen.

My own personal prayer life is a must! However, corporate prayer and praying with others is important as well. Praying in groups is difficult for some but don't be intimidated by how others pray. Start where you are and don't be afraid to be unique. If your heart is open, the Lord will guide you into what He wants for you. This book is simply a testimony of my journey. Hopefully some of it will minister to your life, but some of it you may not put in your suitcase.

> Don't be intimidated by how others pray.

Years ago Heeth and I were involved in a ministry that met in homes and was a very close knit group. Unfortunately, over the course of time, some of those put in leadership were not mature enough to handle the authority given to them. In the midst of some difficult situations, the Lord began to impress on me: "PRAYER, PRAYER, PRAYER!" I began to saturate my mind and spirit with learning more about prayer. I went to the Word, of course, but I also searched out some excellent books such as *Answers to Prayer* by George Mueller, *Destined for the Throne* by Paul Billheimer, *How To Pray* by R.A. Torrey, and *Intercessor* by Reese Howell.

PRAYER PARTNERS

After a time of saturation, I asked the Lord, "What do I do now?" He had me call a friend in our church, and we began to meet once a week. She had small children and I would arrive at her home just as she was putting them down for a nap. We began praying immediately and prayed for one hour. Then I would leave. We did this for about a year and then another friend joined us. It is not necessarily the length of time that you pray. The key is obedience. We did not try to solve all the problems of our group, plus we all had other things we needed to be doing. Those two ladies are still two of my dearest friends. Praying together not only builds a closer relationship with the Lord but also with each other.

I am so blessed every week watching the Tuesday morning prayer at Glory of Zion in Denton, Texas. It is on the web for an hour at 6:00 am and what a powerful hour! It can be watched "on demand" throughout the week as well. Another hour of prayer is webcast on Wednesdays at noon. This is a wonderful way to see the Spirit move and to hear what the Lord is saying in this hour.

Another good source for watching prayer via webcast is the International House of Prayer in Kansas City, KS. I have a special interest in this because my granddaughter is a Bible School student there.

THE POWER OF AGREEMENT

Praying in groups is a powerful tool as Jesus taught about the prayer of agreement in Matthew 18:19-20: *"Again I say to you that if two of you agree on earth concerning anything that they ask, it will be done for them by My Father in heaven. For where two or three are gathered together in My name, I am there in the midst of them."*

As I was pursuing my journey of prayer, the Lord provided a prayer group that was perfect for my next step of training. We came together once a week with no set agenda except to sit at His feet and minister to Him. It was a great season learning to wait on the Lord and to hear His voice.

There is no perfect prayer group as there are no perfect people, but God uses all things for good if we allow Him to do so. In the body of Christ we are a part of the whole body, but your part is important in order for the whole to function. We can read about this in Ephesians 4:16: "*From whom the whole body, joined and knit together by what every joint supplies, according to the effective working by which every part does its share, causes growth of the body for the edifying of itself in love."*

Volumes have been written about prayer. My purpose has been to share with you a very small part of my personal experiences in the area of prayer. I know from many years of walking with the Lord that prayer works. Are there prayers that did not get answered the way I wanted? Yes! Are there things that happened that I do not understand? Yes! However, I know one thing. The Lord is ever faithful, and He has not and will not ever forsake you or me. Prayer moves mountains that may be blocking the highway on our journey. Nothing is impossible for God. Let's keep praying and moving ahead.

> Prayer moves mountains that may be blocking the highway on our journey.

Chapter 10

STEP 4: FEAR OF MAN VERSUS FEAR OF GOD

*The fear of man brings a snare, But whoever
trusts in the Lord shall be safe.*
Proverbs 29:25

*The fear of the Lord is the beginning of wisdom, And
the knowledge of the Holy One is understanding.*
Proverbs 9:10

These two scriptures are absolutely key to our journey into intimacy. Fear of man - what others think or say about us - is one of the biggest road blocks we face on our pathway. One of the best definitions of fear I have come across is this acronym motivational speaker, Zig Ziglar, uses to describe FEAR:

False
Evidence
Appearing
Real

The devil uses false evidence to make us believe his lies and live in fear.

In the first grade, our class play was the story of the life of a shoemaker and his wife. I so wanted to play the part of the wife, but one of my best friends got the part. At the last minute she became sick and I played her part. What fun I had! There was no fear in me. As I progressed through grammar school, I was in many plays as well as dance and piano recitals. I don't remember being afraid of what people were thinking.

FEAR ENTERS THE PICTURE

However, as I grew older, being part of the popular crowd became very important to me. I sincerely loved people and never wanted to hurt anyone's feelings. I hated snobbery – anybody thinking they were better than someone else. It didn't matter to me who you were. I just wanted you to like me and, therefore, I tried to please everyone.

Entering into high school, my three goals were to be a cheerleader, to receive one of the senior superlatives, and to be chosen to ride on the Rose Show float. In Thomasville, Georgia, which is known as the City of Roses, a rose festival was held every year. One of the girls in the Senior Class was crowned as the Rose Show Queen and some of the other seniors were part of the queen's court.

These were not bad goals but definitely were self-seeking and self-serving. I was not seeking first the kingdom of God and truly didn't have a clue what that meant or how to go about it.

I entered the pageant for Rose Queen and won. On Monday morning following the pageant, I went out of my way to be nice and friendly to everyone. I did not want anyone thinking I was stuck up or proud. I truly wanted to be humble...that part was God's grace.

THE REAL WORLD

I was blessed with many friends in high school, and I was naïve enough to think that everybody liked me as much as I did them. After graduation I attended a women's college, and several of my friends from high school went there as well. In my freshman year, my eyes began to be opened to what many call, "the real world." One of my friends gossiped about me, which caused much hurt and disappointment. The truth came to light like a neon sign: "Jacqueline, everybody does not like you or think you are wonderful."

> Being a people-pleaser is not a godly trait!

Being a people-pleaser is not a godly trait! So, as I began my journey with the Lord, I began to take steps away from the fear of man and toward the fear of God. I have come a long way since then, but not without some skinned knees and bruises along the way.

NO MORE FENCE WALKING

After receiving the baptism of the Holy Spirit, many of my friends could not relate to the person I had come to be, or better yet, the person I desired to be. I struggled as the old me tried to "walk the fence" as the expression goes. However, this was not God's plan for Heeth and me.

I cried many tears during times of loneliness and disappointment over feeling left out of many situations and events. The first Christmas after my new commitment to the Lord, one of my dearest friends did not invite us to her annual Christmas dinner. It had been one of my favorite holiday affairs. My flesh was still alive and well as evidenced by my thinking, *I could have gone out and robbed a bank, committed adultery, or cheated on my income tax and would still have been invited!"* Of course, this is a bit exaggerated, but it reveals how "left out" I felt. In actuality, the Lord wanted me to be freed from having to be a part of everything from my past.

WALK YOUR OWN PATH

The Lord works differently in each of our lives. When some people turn their lives over to the Lord, they are able to walk where I could not: they simply cared less about what people thought. Before we are created in our mother's womb, God has a plan for each of us. In order to fulfill God's plan for my life, which I do believe I am walking out today, my journey involved a lot of sacrifice, training, and continual maturing.

In order to have the fear of God as preeminent in our lives, we must make a conscious decision to die to the fear of man. I once heard someone say, "Whatever you fear is what you are literally bowing your knees to." I suddenly could actually see myself bowing my knees to some man or woman when I had feared what they thought about me. I knew that I did not want to continue doing this. I made a choice that day to bow my knees to the Lord and to Him only.

> Before we are created in our mother's womb, God has a plan for each of us.

Psalm 34 reveals some wonderful benefits of the fear of the Lord: "*The angel of the Lord encamps around those who fear Him and delivers them. Oh fear the Lord, you His saints! There is no want to those who fear Him. Come, you children, listen to me; I will teach you the fear of the Lord.*"

The Holy Spirit will teach us the fear of the Lord if we desire to hear and obey. What freedom it is to be freed from being a man-pleaser!

DANGER ON THE PATH

Fearing man is a dangerous place to walk. Being concerned about pleasing people can actually rob you of your destiny. An example of this is related in 1 Samuel 15 when King Saul was told to destroy all the spoils from his battle, including all the livestock. Instead Saul and the people spared Agag, king of the Amalikies, and the best of the sheep, oxen, fatlings, lambs, and all that was good in their eyes.

> Fearing man is a dangerous place to walk.

When Samuel, the prophet, confronted Saul about his disobedience, Saul responded in verse 24: "*I have sinned, for I have trans-*

gressed the commandment of the Lord because I feared the people and obeyed their voice."

Samuel responded to Saul in verse 26: "*I will not return with you, for you have rejected the word of the Lord and the Lord has rejected you from being king over Israel.*"

Saul was still concerned about his image and wanted Samuel to come with him so that it would appear as though everything was alright. He grabbed Samuel's robe and begged him saying, "*I have sinned, yet honor me now, please, before the elders of my people and before Israel, and return with me that I may worship the Lord your God.*"

Samuel did what Saul had been told to do and killed King Agag. Then he left Saul and never saw him again until his death. Verse 35 says, "*Nevertheless, Samuel mourned for Saul, and the Lord regretted that He had made Saul king over Israel.*"

What a tragedy. Saul had such potential, but he failed to fulfill his destiny because of disobedience to the Word of the Lord. He feared man more than God.

#1 GOAL – PLEASE THE LORD

> If we truly have a fear of God our number one goal will be to please Him.

We each have different weaknesses. What may be a weakness for me might not be a problem for you and vice-versa. The key is that if we truly have a fear of God – an awesome reverence for who He is – then our number one goal will be to please Him.

When I go to speak or teach, my prayer is, "*Lord, let me share what is on Your heart today; not my will but Yours be done. I desire to please You, Lord.*" In doing this, I know that some people will like what I say and others will not.

SERVE ONLY THE MASTER

Our hearts must not be divided, as Jesus said in Luke 16:13: "*No servant can serve two masters; for either he will hate the one and love the other, or else he will be loyal to the one and despise the other. You cannot serve God and mammon.*"

Likewise in Isaiah 29:13, the Lord said: "*…these people draw near with their mouths, and honor Me with their lips, and have removed their hearts far from Me, and their fear toward Me is taught by the commandment of men…*"

TIMES OF TESTING

If we are sincere in our desire to fear God and not man, there will be times of testing. When I first started teaching in the prophetic school at our church, there were times when nobody commented on my teaching. I would drive home saying, "Lord, why didn't anyone say something to me? Was it good or did I mess up?"

Quietly in my spirit I knew the Lord was speaking to me saying, "*Jacqueline, do you trust me or not? Who are you trying to please? Am I not bigger than your mistakes? If I called you to teach this school, will I not give you everything you need to teach it?*"

I would like to tell you that today I am completely free of needing or wanting approval from people, but I am not. Deliverance is a continual process. When I catch myself falling back into the people-pleasing habit, I repent and go on.

DO WHAT JESUS DID

As I grow in my love for the Lord, His approval is truly my main objective. I know that He loves me regardless of what I do or don't do. I, also, know that Jesus said He only did those things He saw the Father doing. So, just as His desire was to do those things that are in the Father's heart, our desire should be the same.

Proverbs 27:21 NIV version reads: "*The crucible for silver and the furnace for gold, but man is tested by the praise he receives.*" Praise tests a person just as high temperatures test metal.

> Praise tests a person just as high temperatures test metal.

Questions you need to ask yourself are: "How does praise affect me? Do I strive to get it?" Our attitude toward praise says a lot about where we are in our walk with the Lord. As people of God, we should stay attuned to our convictions and do what we should do, whether we are praised for it or not.

As we learn to walk in the fear of the Lord, we will begin to live in the awe and reverence of God. Our Lord is loving, compassionate, and full of grace and mercy. But He is also powerful, awesome, holy, and sovereign over all things. Yes, on this journey into intimacy, we must grow in the fear of the Lord. It is truly the way of wisdom.

Now that you have learned the four steps to unlock the hidden mysteries of God on the paths of your journey, be sure to take the time to practice each of these steps:

1. Seek the truth of God's Word.
2. Learn to hear the voice of God.
2. Tap into the power of prayer on a daily basis.
4. Grow in the fear of the Lord.

It is said that it takes 21 days to change a habit. Establish a plan and a pattern that fits your style of communicating and living. Walk it out day by day. Don't try to do everything at once. Small steps repeated over time will create life-changing practices that allow you to continue on your journey with joy and peace.

Chapter 11

SHIFTING INTO THE NEW SEASON

*"Rapid success from a small beginning
will be as sweet as honey!"*
Chuck D. Pierce

It is during seasons of change in our lives that Satan, the enemy of all mankind, lays a trap to try to draw us away from our relationship with the Lord. When I chose to draw closer to the Lord, I entered into battle to withstand the enemy's trap to stir up my emotions regarding the changes taking place within me. I shared in earlier chapters how many relationships shifted because we chose to walk a new path with the Lord. It wasn't that God wanted us to live as hermits or not to enjoy life. He simply was leading us to seek His kingdom

> During seasons of change, Satan lays a trap to draw us away from the Lord.

first and His righteousness. Then all other things would be added to us.

What I didn't understand was that the Lord was shifting me out of the old season into a new beginning. I was reminded of a study I once did of the book of Ruth. To my surprise, the Lord had me focus the study on Naomi rather than Ruth. As a young wife and mother, Naomi suffered through the consequences of famine where she lived in Bethlehem, a city of Judah. In order to feed their family, her husband, Elimelech, decided to move with Naomi and their two sons to the country of Moab. Leaving family and friends to live in a land of strangers must have been very hard for Naomi.

Was this move God's best for them or did they move in fear of lack and provision? It is difficult to tell. Sometime after the move, Elimelech died leaving her with two sons, who eventually married Moabite women, one named Ruth and the other was Orpah. It may not have been Naomi's first choice for her sons to marry outside of the Jewish faith, but Naomi still loved her daughters-in-law.

Ten years later both of Naomi's sons died leaving her with no heirs. In the culture of that time, women left without heirs had no means of support and protection. It was a very serious matter. We can only imagine the grief, fear, and helplessness she felt. She must have wondered how she would find the strength to go on.

Naomi had two choices to make – draw closer to God or draw away from Him and become bitter. We have this same choice when tragedy comes or when we face the everyday problems of life.

MOVING FORWARD

After receiving word that the Lord had blessed His people in Judah with good harvests, Naomi's heart was drawn to return to her homeland. She didn't know what the future held for her, but she did not let her loss keep her from moving forward. She did what she knew to do – follow her heart and the leading of the Lord.

> "Entreat me not to leave you."

As Naomi prepared to leave Moab, she released Ruth and Orpah to return to their families. She wanted these young women to have an opportunity to remarry, have children, and be provided for. Orpah decided to stay in Moab with her family. However, Ruth refused to leave Naomi and said, "*Entreat me not to leave you, or to turn back from following after you; for wherever you lodge, I will lodge; your people shall be my people, and your God, my God."* Naomi and Ruth were shifting into a new beginning together.

When Naomi and Ruth arrived in Bethlehem, everyone was excited to welcome them. Naomi revealed her true emotional state when she said, *"Do not call me Naomi; call me Mara, for the Almighty has dealt very bitterly with me. I went out full, and the Lord has brought me home again empty."*

> How we trust Him during loss is a thermometer of where we are in our journey.

It was apparent that Naomi recognized her grief had turned her heart bitter. It is easy to love and praise the Lord when everything is going well, but it is more difficult to do so in times of trouble. How we trust Him during times of loss is often a thermometer of where we are in our journey.

GOD'S PERFECT TIMING

God knew Naomi's heart toward Him and His compassionate love made a way for her. God's timing was perfect as they arrived at the start of harvest time. He prepared a new beginning for Naomi and Ruth both in the natural and in the spiritual. As Naomi went into this new season, she could have remained bitter and angry at

God for the deaths of her husband and sons. She could have put all of her trust and security in Ruth alone. Instead, as she unselfishly watched over Ruth and guided her into a new beginning with a husband and child, Naomi was set free from her bitterness. As the Scriptures tell us, Ruth married Boaz and became the mother of Obed, who was the father of Jesse, the father of King David and the lineage of Jesus.

DON'T DESPISE SMALL BEGINNINGS

Heeth and I were excited to attend the Head of the Year Conference at Glory of Zion in Denton, Texas in September of 2009. The three-day conference was being held on a 31-acre tract of land just north of the city along Highway 35E. This event, also, marked the final payment being made on the land purchased by Glory of Zion.

A large tent to seat over 2,000 people and three smaller tents – all of which were on raised platforms and air conditioned - were erected to house the meetings, concessions and a bookstore. North Texas had been experiencing severe drought, but the week before the planned event, the heavens opened and rain saturated the land. The resulting wind and mud put unexpected hurdles in the path of those preparing for this gathering. However, it did not stop them from moving forward and putting contingency plans in place for roadways to be reinforced, alternatives arranged for parking off site, and obtaining vans and busses to transport attendees and volunteer workers on and off the property.

Chuck Pierce, president of Glory of Zion, shared the following segment in a 40-day prayer focus he sent out during this time. He asked his wife, Pam, to write what the Spirit of God was sharing with her, and here is what she wrote:

> "I was standing outside in the rain after Chuck left for the office. As the much-needed moisture soaked through my shirt, I looked up at the sky and said, '*Lord, what's up with all the rain? This really makes things difficult for the Head of the Year Conference out on the land.*' I didn't have to wait long for God's answer in my spirit. The Lord said, '*You don't get to choose when I decide to break the drought in this region.*'"

> "Well that was enough of an explanation for me! The mud, while an inconvenience for us, is a minor hurdle in God's plan for the land and for

His people. I believe we all have the opportunity to please Him with our response to the weather over the next few days. As for me, I'm wearing jeans and my rain boots!"

Chuck continued this dialogue in the prayer focus:

"My son, Joseph, then walked in my office after I read Pam's email. He and Ethan, my seventeen year old, had been part of the 1-3 AM Prayer Watch in the big tent on the land. While they were praying, they looked up and saw a hummingbird in the tent."

"Pam called me while Joseph was telling me about this and said, '*Oh my, I am watching the rain outside my kitchen window, and I see a hummingbird hovering and watching me!*' I went to find prophetically what this meant. Here is the significance: 'Rapid success from a small beginning will be as sweet as honey!'"

> "Rapid success from a small beginning will be as sweet as honey!"

"Here is what I hear the Lord saying to each of us as we end the last season. Ask Him to break your drought! Let Him send you refreshing in His way and in His timing. Then in the midst of the new that is beginning around you, do not despise small beginnings. Lift up your eyes around you and LOOK, for there are signs very near you. The season ahead is about LOOKING BEYOND AND SEEING WHAT YOU COULD NOT SEE IN THE LAST SEASON."[1]

Heeth and I were amazed at how the celebration of the land purchase and the conference moved ahead in spite of the rain and mud. It was a time of refreshing, joy, and revelation for all who attended.

Your journey into intimacy may be a small beginning, but you can taste the sweetness if you will come aside and sup with the Master. I AM is answering your prayers and will show you a *new* and *different* way to get over the ruts in the road that may have tripped you up in the past.

ADVANCE PREPARATION

In our journey into intimacy, we will face difficult and sometimes tragic circumstances. We must learn how to look and see beyond what we have seen in the past season. Then, we must exercise our faith against the enemy in order to move forward into a place of new beginnings as Naomi and Ruth did. A close intimate relationship with the Lord is the rock we can cling to in troubled times.

We must be prepared for each season of life *before* crisis comes. Preparation takes place line upon line and precept upon precept. We each have a uniquely different testimony. It is never too late until the day that we die to shift closer to God. The choice is ours.

Chapter 12

CONSIDERING THE CALL

But those who wait (hope) on the Lord Shall renew their strength; They shall mount up with wings like eagles, They shall run and not be weary, They shall walk and not faint.
Isaiah 40:31

During the summer of 2009 Heeth and I spent a week in Wyoming enjoying the Teton Mountains with our oldest daughter and her husband. As I gazed at the beauty and majesty of the mountains, it caused me to praise the Lord for what He had created.

I have often compared my walk with the Lord to climbing a mountain. The walk began at the bottom of the mountain when I

> As we ascend into a more intimate relationship with the Lord it is always a temptation to stop where we are.

said, "Yes, to His call." Then as I began the climb – step by step – some of the climb was easy, some of it was rocky, and some steps were very hard. In this life we never reach the top, because there is always more to learn and experience. However, as we ascend and come into a more intimate relationship with the Lord, it is always a temptation to stop and set up camp where we are. We, also, have the choice of returning to where we started.

DON'T MISS THE CALL

A number of years ago when my youngest daughter and her husband lived in Colorado, we took a mountain hike together as a family. Rand is an excellent guide and carefully led us up the mountain. After several hours we were all ready for lunch. When we arrived at a beautiful area, we told Rand that we wanted to stop there. He responded, "No, we must go a little further. This is not the place to have lunch." None of us were happy with his decision, but we continued to walk. Sometime later, we arrived at a spot so gorgeous that it would be impossible to describe. I have thought many times what we would have missed if we had stopped and not continued up the mountain as Rand insisted.

It is the same in our walk with the Lord. We can stop anywhere along the way. We will still get to heaven, but we may miss the call and destiny the Lord had planned for us if we stop too soon.

There is a call going out across the land to seek the Lord with all of our hearts and to walk in His ways. He is challenging us in these exciting and sober times. As the natural world appears to be growing darker and darker, the kingdom of God will shine brighter and brighter in the midst of the darkness. The intensity of the warfare is in-

> God desires that each of us willingly accept the call to fulfill our destiny in Christ.

creasing, but God has promised to make a way where there seems to be no way. This makes it more and more critical to draw closer to the Lord to be able to enter into His secret place of intimacy with Him.

A CALL FROM THE FATHER'S HEART

God desires that each of us willingly accept the call to fulfill our destiny in Christ. There is a call being issued from the Father through His Son. Jesus is saying, "Come and follow Me." It is both an invitation and a command to become like Christ and to embrace His desires for the world. This call originates from the Father's heart.

Intimacy with God is the pathway of preparation for entering into this new dimension of the Spirit.

> Often doors are closed in our lives because we did not take the time to prepare in advance.

The *Webster's Ninth New Collegiate Dictionary* defines *prepare* as "to make ready beforehand for some purpose, use or activity."[1] The Hebrew word for "prepare" is *kown*, which means to be erect (stand perpendicular); certainty; confirm; faithfulness, be fixed; be stable, perfect. The root of the word in Hebrew is the same as consecrate, dedicated to a sacred purpose. In other words, we need to make ourselves ready to fulfill a dedicated, sacred purpose.

BE PREPARED

When thinking about the importance of preparation, I am reminded of the parable of the wise and foolish virgins in Matthew 25:1-13. The story tells us that ten virgins went out to meet the bridegroom. Five of them were foolish because they took their lamps but had no extra oil with them. The five wise virgins took extra oil and were prepared no matter how long it took for the bridegroom to come. When the bridegroom tarried, the oil in the lamps of the foolish virgins was used up. While the foolish virgins went to buy more oil, the bridegroom came. Those who were ready, went into the wedding chamber, and the door was closed.

Often doors are closed in our lives because we did not take the time to prepare in advance.

SHAKE IT OFF AND STEP UP

I came across a story of an old mule that had fallen in a well and couldn't get out. The farmer decided it was impossible to haul the mule out of the well so some of his friends came to help him fill in the well. As the farmers shoveled dirt onto the mule, he suddenly realized that if he shook off the dirt and stepped up, he would eventually be able to get out of the well. Through the darkness and panic of the dirt pouring down on him, the mule kept saying over and over, "Shake it off and step up!" As he continued to follow this process, he did finally step out onto solid ground. Likewise, we must shake off those things that are trying

We must continually speak His Word to overcome seemingly impossible circumstances.

to defeat us and hinder our walk and step up onto the solid Word of the Lord.

As the old mule became weary of having to shake off the dirt and step up over and over and over, he knew if he didn't overcome the temptation to give up, he would die. This is a picture of how we are to encourage ourselves in the Lord. We must continually speak His Word to overcome seemingly impossible circumstances.

The Invitation To The Wedding

Jesus gave the parable of the marriage feast, which is recorded in Matthew 22, to illustrate that while many are called, few will respond. Today, as the Lord is calling His people to make themselves ready, many will refuse to obey the call.

This parable also points out an important detail of the Jewish marriage custom. Wedding hosts sent out two wedding invitations. The first was sent far in advance to let people know that a wedding was being prepared and they would be invited. This was necessary because weddings were major events that lasted as long as a week, and many had to travel long distances to attend. Furthermore, it took time for the replies to come back.

When all the preparations were complete, messengers were sent out with a second invitation telling the guests that the feast was ready, and it was time for the celebration to begin. To turn down that second invitation, which was the one the guest in the parable refused, constituted not merely bad manners but was considered a rejection of the host family's hospitality and an insult to their dignity.

Many in the church who have accepted Jesus as their Savior are not willing to pay the price to make Him their Lord. He is not first in their lives, and they are not prepared to respond to the call of the Bridegroom. For those who are willing, the Holy Spirit will give instructions and guidance for further preparation before it is too late.

> We are coming to a time when there will be no more "fence sitting."

Which Side Am I On?

We are coming to a time when there will be no more "fence sitting." It will be necessary to make a choice to either work for the Lord or against Him. Therefore, we must now lay aside things that would hinder our walk with Him.

One of my favorite scriptures is Hebrews 12:1: *"Therefore we also, since we are surrounded by such a cloud of witnesses, let us lay aside every weight, and the sin which so easily ensnares us, and let us run with endurance the race that is set before us."*

This is simply – asking the Lord – "Is there anything in my life that is distracting me from Your best?"

BE STRONG AND OF GOOD COURAGE

You may desire to be closer to the Lord but question if you have the strength or courage to accept His call.

> We possess all that is necessary to do His will.

My response would be, "In Christ we are overcomers, and our love for Him is the only force great enough to preserve us and to lift us up to Him. We must not forget that we stand beside the all powerful Christ. Therefore, we possess all that is necessary to do His will as it says in Philippians 4:13, *'I can do all things through Christ who strengthens me.'*"

As you now are moving forward to accept the call, believe that you are not alone. Abba Father is standing with you.

Chapter 13

ACCEPTING THE CALL

Hours with God make minutes
with man more effective.

Are you now ready to accept His call? The only safe place for God's people is continually seeking to progress in spiritual things. Paul called the vision and goal that was set before him, "the mark for the prize of the high calling of God in Christ Jesus."

My special readers: As we have progressed together on this journey, let's stop a moment and reflect on these two points:

1. No two people's journey is ever the same.

2. Some of the things that you will read in this chapter may be unfamiliar to you. Just remember to only put in your suitcase what is right for you at this time.

Now pray this prayer as paraphrased from Ephesians 1:17-19: "*Lord, flood me with the spirit of wisdom and revelation in the knowledge of You, let the eyes of my understanding be enlightened, that I may know what is the hope of Your calling, what are the riches of the glory of Your inheritance in the saints, and what is the exceedingly greatness of Your power toward us who believe, according to the working of Your mighty power.*"

DO WHAT JESUS DID

The New Testament apostles experienced the power of God in their lives *because they were intimate with God* giving themselves continually to prayer and to the ministry of the Word. After Jesus' ascension to the Father and the coming of the power of the Holy Spirit upon them at Pentecost, the apostles began teaching and operating in miracles, signs, and wonders. Crowds of people began following them just as they had Jesus, and the church multiplied in numbers daily.

Needless to say, the chief priests and elders of the synagogue were upset and began to threaten the apostles and believers about teaching in the name of Jesus. Much to the chagrin of the synagogue leaders, the apostles refused to listen to the voice of man and pressed forward - no matter what the cost. The anointing of the Holy Spirit was so strong that the apostles were of one heart and one soul moving with great power and boldness. When the apostles continued to heal and do miracles, the high priest had them thrown in prison, but an angel came and opened the prison doors. They returned to the temple and continued to preach and teach and heal in Jesus' name.

> The apostles experienced the power of God because they were intimate with God.

The priests again brought the apostles before the temple council and had them beaten, commanding them not to speak of Jesus. In Acts 5:41-42 we read: "*So they departed from the presence of the council, **rejoicing** that they were counted worthy to suffer shame for His name. And daily in the temple and in every house, they did not cease teaching and preaching Jesus as the Christ.*"

JOY AND CONFIDENCE IN THE GREAT I AM

The apostles had lived and served *intimately* with Jesus day and night for three and one-half years. Each had given up everything to follow Him. Now they prepared to serve Him with joy. They *knew* the great I AM, and as we have just read, they refused to stop doing what He had commissioned them to do. They had shifted into a new dimension of power and authority that was unstoppable. Such monumental change would not have been possible without the power of the Holy Spirit and their willing acceptance of the apostolic call upon their lives.

> God is our strength and our source of joy.

It is very key to note that the apostles were able to rejoice that they were counted worthy to suffer for His name. This was not a natural thing but supernatural, made possible by their obedience.

Philippians 4:4 tells us to *"Rejoice in the Lord always. Again I say rejoice."* It is interesting to note that Paul was in prison when he wrote the book of Philippians.

The world around us seems to be getting darker and darker, but God is our strength and the source of our joy. As it says in Nehemiah 8:10b, *"The joy of the Lord is your strength."*

He is such a wonderful Lord. No matter how bleak things may seem, His peace and joy are available to us by His Spirit.

Prepare to Walk In His Call

As a member of the body of Christ, the question we must be ready to answer is: What must I do to prepare to walk into this new dimension of God's kingdom work?

Answering this question requires a willingness to make four sincere commitments.

1. **Be receptive to and value what God is doing in our day:**

   David's army included the sons of Issachar who had an understanding of the times to know what Israel ought to do in the time of battle. Likewise, it is very important that we also understand what the Lord is doing today. Then we must be obedient with the revelation and impartation that we have been given.

2. **Desire to be a part of what God is doing:**

   As we read earlier, the apostles empowered by the Holy Spirit were fully committed and in one accord with one another and with God. We must be in one accord without wavering in what God is revealing to us to do. James 1:8 says that *a double minded man is unstable in all his ways*. Like an army if we accept this call, we will lay down our desires and rise to the command of the Lord of Hosts.

3. Be committed to act on what God is doing:

> Our ears must be open to the heavenly sound of our day.

If we believe in what God is doing, we must express ourselves in faith with corresponding action. James 2:26 says, "*For as the body without the spirit is dead, so faith without works is dead also.*"

4. Be sensitive to the call:

We each have a place in God's plan. We must be alert and hear His call whenever it comes in order to be in the right place at the right time. Our ears must be open to the heavenly sound of our day. This call is beyond the realm of "business as usual." As Jesus says, "Follow Me," He is echoing the Father's heart.

THE PATTERN OF JESUS

Jesus said in John 5:30, "*I can of Myself do nothing. As I hear, I judge; and My judgment is righteous, because I do not seek My own will but the will of the Father who sent Me.*" Jesus did only those things the Father told Him to do. Apart from the Father, He did nothing.

That must be our pattern – to seek and do only those things which the Spirit reveals are the Father's heart.

In Henry Blackaby's book, *Experiencing God*, he shares that we are to watch to see where God is working and join Him.[1] Unfortunately, often the opposite is true. We make our plans and then ask the Lord to bless them.

JESUS – THE LIGHT OF THE WORLD

The circumstances in which we walk cannot cause us to be in fear. We must put our faith and confidence in His Word as it says in John 8:12, "*I am the light of the world. He who follows Me shall not walk in darkness, but have the light of life.*"

Christ is the true Light and it is our joy to follow Him. It is not enough to look at the light and just gaze upon it. We must follow it, believe in it, and walk in it.

For it is a light to our feet, not to our eyes only.[2] The Bride who follows after her Bridegroom does not walk in darkness. She has the Light of life – and everlasting life in the world to come.

CALLED TO HOLINESS

We are called to be a holy people because God is holy as I Peter 1:13-16 tells us: *"Therefore gird up the loins of your mind, be sober, and rest your hope fully upon the grace that is to be brought to you at the revelation of Jesus Christ; as obedient children, not conforming yourselves to the former lusts, as in your ignorance; but as He who called you is holy, you also be holy in all your conduct, because it is written, 'Be Holy, for I am holy.'"*

> Being holy is not being religious.

Being holy is not being religious. It simply means putting His desires above our own desires and turning away from that which the world demands. It means living according to the will of God. The holy person is always alert, keeping his mind clear, fit for his walk with God.

LISTENING FOR THE TRUMPET CALL

Paul warned the church about giving an "uncertain sound" in I Corinthians 14:8: *"For if the trumpet makes an uncertain sound, who will prepare for battle?"*

In the Old Testament, the number of trumpet sounds indicated what was to be done, whether to gather for war or for worship. Hearing the clear sound of the trumpet, alerts us to the Holy Spirit's call and directions. When there is a failure to produce a clear call, no one is sure if or when he needs to be ready.

> Hearing the clear sound of the trumpet, alerts us to the Holy Spirit's call and directions.

In Old Testament days the people were trained to hear and obey the sound of the trumpet. They were taught by their leaders what the sounds indicated and how to respond.

One of the commitments that we mentioned earlier was to be receptive to and value what God is doing today. In order to do this, we must first understand what the Lord is saying to us individually and through His prophets and other leaders in this period of time. Then we have a responsibility to respond to the revelation that we have been given.

ALWAYS A REMNANT

Over the centuries many have fallen away and turned to the way of carnality, but there is always a remnant that does not recognize defeat. They are the ones who hold fast when others run away.[3]

There always have been those who stand when others fall. When Lucifer broke rank in heaven and set himself up against the Almighty God, Gabriel and Michael did not waver. When it was time to enter into the Promised Land, Joshua and Caleb were the only ones bold enough to say, "Let's go in and possess the land." The others trembled in fear of the giants that stood between them and the promise of God. The three Hebrew children in Babylon faced the deadly flames of the furnace rather than bow to an impotent idol. Daniel went into the lions' den

> There always have been those who stand when others fall.

rather than submit to the king's commands not to pray to God.

There remains a remnant *"being kept by the power of God through faith for salvation ready to be revealed in the last time,"* as it says in I Peter 1:5. We must be totally at rest in the assurance that it is His power that will protect and prepare us in the days to come.

Those that seek first His face will hear the call of the Bridegroom. By their love for Him and their willingness to pay the price of preparation, they will be His lights in those days. The light of His Spirit, reflected in the Bride, will draw many out of darkness. As the Bride is waiting with her eyes on eternal things, her life is not wasted. He will use her as she waits, and she will be doing only those things that follow the Father's heart.

> True fulfillment comes as we walk out our destiny in Christ.

This is a very important key: The Bride is busy doing the things that the Lord has called her to do. Each person's assignment will be different. True fulfillment comes as we walk out our destiny in Christ.

May our response be, "Father, take our lives and let them be totally set apart for YOU! We are not our own." Let this be the fulfillment of our journey into intimacy as we stand firm, readily accepting His call.

Conclusion

A PASSION FOR INTIMACY

Deep calls unto deep at the noise of Your waterfalls;
All Your waves and billows have gone over me.

Psalm 42:7

As you have begun your own journey into intimacy while reading this book, my prayer is that you have been touched by Him in greater measure and have developed a burning passion to know Him more. The Lord desires to have such an intimate relationship with us that we can be as one with Him.

> The Lord desires to have such an intimate relationship with us that we can be as one with Him.

Jesus prayed for each of us, in the garden of Gethsemane on the night He was betrayed with such fervor that it was said He sweated blood. Meditate on His words from John

17:20-23 and let them sink into your heart: *"I do not pray for these alone, but also for those who will believe in Me through their word; that they all may be one, as You, Father, are in Me, and I in You; that they also may be one in Us, that the world may believe that You sent Me. And the glory which You gave Me I have given them, that they may be one just as We are one: I in them, and You in Me; that they may be made perfect in one, and that the world may know that You have sent Me, and have loved them as You have loved Me."*

Jesus has actually given us His glory. He expressed His love for us with such intensity thousands of years before we were even born, because He wanted us to come into complete unity and fullness with Him. That is how passionate He is about being intimate with us.

As we behold the glory of the Lord, we with increasing glory reflect what we behold. The apostle Paul wrote of this glory in II Corinthians 3:18, *"But we all, with unveiled face, beholding as in a mirror the glory of the Lord, are being transformed into the same image from glory to glory, just as by the Spirit of the Lord."*

A proper understanding of God's dealings in life comes only by knowing His perspective and ways. This calls for great patience, but

God made a way for us as we read in Isaiah 40:31: *"But they that wait upon the Lord shall renew their strength; they shall mount up with wings as eagles, they shall run and not be weary; and they shall walk and not faint."*

As we wait upon the Lord, we go about the routines of life with a fervent and patient hope that He will consummate His rule in His time. This attitude within us gives us strength to see beyond the moment.

> A proper understanding of God's dealings in life comes only by knowing His perspective and ways.

The prayer that we must pray is, "Draw me." Then we must make the commitment to the Lord that the Shulamite maiden made in Song of Solomon: "We will run after You."

As we ask the Lord to enlarge our spiritual hunger and establish our consecration to follow Him alone, our Heavenly Bridegroom becomes active within us and in our circumstances. This will change us into the Bride He longingly desires us to be.

As His Bride, we are a "chosen" generation, a royal priesthood, an holy nation, a peculiar people; that we should show forth the praises of Him who has called us out of darkness into His marvelous light (paraphrased from I Peter 2:9 KJV). God's intention from the time of Abraham has been to call forth a people with a special mission – to proclaim His praise and propagate His blessing throughout the earth.

Great men and women have written about experiences of overwhelming intimacy with God. One commentator noted: "I never seemed to be so unhinged from myself and so wholly devoted to God. My heart was swallowed up in God most of the day."[1] Perhaps this is the heart of all worship, the center of God's desire for us today.

The Psalms of David are filled with the heart-cry of a man who sought a deep personal relationship with the Lord, Himself. Again and again, David expressed a burning desire to intimately know the Lord on two levels of experience:

1. **As one with whom he could come face-to-face:**

   Deep calls unto deep at the noise of Your waterfalls; All Your waves and billows have gone over me.

   Psalm 42:7

As the deer pants for the water brooks, so pants my soul for You, O God. My soul thirsts for God for the living God. When shall I come and appear before God.

Psalm 42:1-2

2. As one in whom he could place infinite trust:

In God have I put my trust; I will not be afraid. What can man do to me?

Psalm 56:11

The Lord is my light and my salvation; Whom shall I fear? The Lord is the strength of my life; Of whom shall I be afraid?

Psalm 27:1

David came into a relationship with the Lord in which he had many experiences of receiving the portion of wisdom, provision, or protection that was needed during difficult times. As a result, a deep trust in the Lord resided in David.

God is no respecter of persons. He is saying to us today, "Come Walk With Me." He is offering to us the same relationship He had with David; one of face-to-face confidant and one of wisdom, protector, and provider. The Lord is calling us to a level of intimacy that will give us overcoming power to stand firm in His love no matter what comes against us.

> The Lord is calling us to a level of intimacy that will give us overcoming power.

I hope you have gained insight for your own walk with the Lord and will stay on His pathway of intimacy because the journey never ends. It just becomes more and more exciting as we move from deep unto deep and from glory unto glory. May the Lord bless you mightily as you seek more of Him, moment by moment and day by day.

EPILOGUE

Almost forty years have passed since the Lord baptized me with the Holy Spirit. Forty years in biblical terminology is considered a generation. In 1970 I was the mother of four young children. Today Heeth and I are blessed with ten precious grandchildren. Our Lord is the God of generations. As I told you earlier about the prayer time with my oldest granddaughter, in this hour the Lord is calling for the generations to minister together. We need each other.

The world is full of chaos and many people are fearful of the unknown. However, the Lord has not changed. He is the same yesterday, today, and forever. There is no shadow of turning with Him.

No price is too great to pay to follow His will. Even in the darkest of hours, He is there. In John 12:3 we read, "*Then Mary took a pound of very costly spikenard, anointed the feet of Jesus and wiped His feet with her hair.*" This is the same Mary that had sat at His feet, while her sister Martha was busy with many things. Mary had come to love Him and in her eyes there was no price too great to pay to please and worship her Lord. In Jesus' day that precious oil was equal in value to a year's wages. In today's retail market a pound of pure spikenard oil could cost over $700.

Matthew's account of this story in Chapter 26:6-9 reads, *"And when Jesus was in Bethany at the house of Simon the leper, a woman came to Him having an alabaster flask of very costly fragrant oil, and she poured it on His head as He sat at the table. But when His disciples saw it, they were indignant, saying, 'Why this waste? For this fragrant oil might have been sold for much and given to the poor.'"*

Jesus rebuked His disciples for criticizing Mary for giving extravagantly to bless Him. He knew she was anointing Him for burial, though His acknowledgement of this went right over the heads of the disciples at that time. This was the turning point for Judas Iscariot, and in anger he went to the chief priests, betraying Jesus for 30 pieces of silver.

We must grow in the confidence in the Christ within us. As we hear His voice and walk in obedience to His will, pleasing Him must be our number one desire. There will always be those that do not understand. Remember we must walk in a fear of a holy God and not fear of man.

FOR THE EYES OF THE Lord run to and fro throughout the whole earth, to show Himself strong on behalf of those whose heart is loyal to Him. He is looking for those that will be His lights in the midst of the troubled world around us. In John 8:12 Jesus tells us "*I am the light of the world. He who follows Me shall not walk in darkness, but have the light of life.*"

So the Lord's question to you would be, "Will you be My light in this hour? Are you willing to pay the price?"

No matter where you are in your walk with the Lord, there is always another step to take. You may have read this book and just decided to begin your walk with Him. Or, you may have been walking with Him for years — the key is continuing to embrace what He is doing in this hour. Remember He has already prepared everything that you will need for the journey. He is simply extending an invitation to you saying, "*Come Walk With Me.*" The price is costly but the reward is beyond measure if you accept His call.

END NOTES

Chapter 2

[1]*Great Grace*, Words & Music by John Dickson, Aaron Smith and Tiffany Smith.

[2] Strong, *Greek Dictionary of the New Testament,* p. 36.

[3] Varnedoe. p. 28.

Chapter 3

[1]Ten Boom. *Plenty for Everyone*, p. 48.

[2]Ten Boom. *Amazing Love*, p. 8.

[3]Ibid.

[4]Morgan, p. 282.

[5]Ibid.

[6]Ibid.

Chapter 4

[1] Salem, p.130.

Chapter 5

[1]Morgan, p. 220.

[2] Pierce, p. 39.

[3] Ibid, p. 40.

Chapter 6

[1] *Webster's New World,* p. 766.

[2] Rodale, p. 593.

[3] Salem, p. 129.

[4] Chavda, p. 7.

[5] Ibid, p. 54.

Chapter 11

Pierce, Chuck. *Prayer Focus,* Day 24.

Chapter 12

[1] *Webster's Ninth,* p. 929.

Chapter 13

[1] Blackaby, p. 15.

[2] Hamon, p.234.

[3] Smith, p. 35.

Conclusion

[1] Edward.

BIBLIOGRAPHY

Blackaby, Henry & King, Claude V. *Experiencing God*. Lifeway Press. 1990.

Chavda, Mahesh. *The Hidden Power of Speaking in Tongues*. Destiny Image Publishers, Inc.: Shippensburg, PA. 2003.

Edward, Jonathan (ed.). *Life and Diary of David Brainerd*. Baker Books. 1989.

Hamon, Bill. *Apostles, Prophets, and the Coming Moves of God*. Destiny Image Publishers, Inc.: Shippensburg, PA. 1996.

Great Grace, Words & Music by John Dickson, Aaron Smith and Tiffany Smith: Glory of Zion International Ministries, Inc.: Denton, TX. 2008.

Morgan, Robert J. *Then Sings My Soul*. Thomas Nelson, Inc.: Nashville, TN. 2003.

Pierce, Chuck D. & Pamela J. *One Thing*. Destiny Image Publishers, Inc.: Shippensburg, PA. 2006.

Pierce, Chuck D. *40 Days of Revamping and Revitalizing Prayer Focus*. www.Glory of Zion International.com 2009.

Rodale, J. I. *The Synonym Finder*. Warner Books: New York, NY. 1978.

Salem, Harry & Cheryl. *Being #1 at Being #2*. Harrison House: Tulsa, OK. 1998.

Smith, Linda. *God's Wife-The Bride of Christ*. Free Them Ministries, Inc. 1977.

Strong, James, LL.D, S.T.D. *The New Strong's Exhaustive Concordance of the Bible: Greek Dictionary of the New Testament*. Thomas Nelson Publishers: Nashville, TN. 1984.

Ten Boom, Corrie. *Amazing Love*. Christian Literature Crusade: Fort Washington, PA. 1953.

Ten Boom, Corrie. *Plenty for Everyone*. Christian Literature Crusade: Fort Washington, PA. 1967.

Varnedoe, Heeth, III. *Called to Excellence*. Evergreen Press: Mobile, AL. 2006.

Webster's Ninth New Collegiate Dictionary. Mirriam-Webster Inc.: Springfield, MA. 1986.

Webster's New World Dictionary of the American Language. The World Publishing Company: New York, NY. 1960.

ABOUT THE AUTHOR

Jacqueline Varnedoe carries a prophetic mantel and anointing to challenge God's people with the truth and to manifest the grace to do what the Bible says they can do. The Lord has given her a mandate to help His Bride make Herself ready and come into the fullness of His power for the days ahead.

In her book, *Come Away With Me...A Journey Into Intimacy*, Jacqueline stirs up in God's people a greater hunger for intimacy and passion for the Lord. She believes that God is raising up a body of believers that must be prepared to maintain spiritual intimacy in the midst of difficulties, disappointment, and perhaps even persecution.

In 1995, Jacqueline founded and has since taught a three-part series of prophetic schools at New Covenant in Thomasville, Georgia and at other churches in the area. In the ensuing years, many people have been motivated and energized in their gifts by attending these schools.

Jacqueline and her husband, Heeth Varnedoe III, founded the ministry, Calling to Excellence, to help equip, train, and activate the saints in their gifts and callings.

Jacqueline Ponder married Heeth Varnedoe III in 1960 after graduating from the University of Georgia with a Bachelor of Arts degree. Jacqueline was ordained into ministry with Christian International (CI) in 1996 and received her Master's in Biblical Studies with CI in 1999. Jacqueline and Heeth serve on the Board of Governors of CI. They reside in Thomasville, GA.

ABOUT MARGIE KNIGHT

For more than 20 years Margie Knight has been turning dreams into accomplished goals. Margie believes she is called to be a "servant to the servants of the Lord" and is gifted in capturing the anointing and style of authors as she writes and edits their work. KnightWriter-2-Publish, is the Lord's vehicle to utilize her gifts for His kingdom as she helps others reach a higher level of success in their own kingdom callings.

With its complete turnkey approach to writing, editing and publishing, KnightWriter-2-Publish offers the services necessary to turn an author's ideas or manuscript into a quality product.

With more than 25 book projects successfully completed, KnightWriter-2-Publish commits to total customer satisfaction for every project. Margie says, "Your goals are our goals as we match your vision to bring you success."

For more information contact Margie Knight at: KnightWriter2publish@gmail.com

To order additional copies of

Come Walk with Me

Email: KnightWriter2publish@gmail.com